MW01676423

NicE
THE GUIDE

HERITAGE SITES, MUSEUMS,
THEMED WALKS AROUND NICE

Adapted from the French and translated by

Jane Bradshaw

For Marjie who loved going to the Negresco

MÉMOIRES MILLÉNAIRES
éditions

CONTENTS

Not to be missed Heritage Sites and Museums

Themed Walks

HERITAGE SITES, MUSEUMS,
THEMED WALKS AROUND NICE

ÉDITIONS MÉMOIRES MILLÉNAIRES

« For a living heritage »

Tél. : +33 (0)4 93 17 75 52 - memoiresmillenaires@wanadoo.fr
132 avenue de la mer - 06700 Saint-Laurent-du-Var
FRANCE

www.memoiresmillenaires.com

A BRIEF HISTORY OF NICE

Nice has a long and complex history. Some significant periods are:

Prehistory: 400,000 years ago, groups of hunters stayed regularly in a cove at Terra Amata. Traces of their campfires can be seen at the Museum of the same name. Then, 170,000 years ago, the nearby Lazaret cave was used to shelter families of hominids (*Homo erectus*). Prehistorians consider Nice to be a site of major scientific interest.

Antiquity: *Nikaïa* (Nice) was founded in the 3rd century B.C. by Greek sea-faring traders from *Massalia* (Marseille). In the 1st century B.C., the Romans established *Cemenelum* (Cimiez), capital of the Province of the *Alpes-Maritimae*. By the 3rd century A.D. its population had reached 30,000, whereas Nice was still a simple port (*Portus Nicaeesium*).

The Middle Ages: This was a long period of turbulence. After repeated invasions, Cemenelum, was abandoned in the 7th century. The incursions continued through the centuries with the arrival of the Saracens. The region, including Nice, was freed by the Count of Provence (972). From the 13th century, the hilltop castle of Nice (*Château*) was extended and enclosed by ramparts, along with the town and its cathedral. In 1388, during the War for the Succession of Provence, Nice placed itself under the protection of the House of Savoy.

Since the 16th century: Nice's destiny has been closely tied to its relations with France. In 1543, the Château resisted a siege by the Franco-Turkish alliance, after which Nice decided to move its civilian population down to the plain (*Ville Basse*), investing the hilltop fortress with a purely military role (*Ville Haute*). By the end of the 17th century, Nice had acquired the reputation of being one of Europe's most formidable forts. Its capture in 1705, after two sieges by the army of Louis XIV, King of France, was not expected. Before returning Nice to the House of Savoy, he ordered the demolition of the *Château de Nice* and the fortress town. Nice was taken again during the French Revolution (1792) and returned, in 1814, to the Duke of Savoy, now the King of Piedmont-Sardinia. From that time on, the town enjoyed a long period of peace. The first aristocratic and wealthy tourists, began to arrive, initially from Great Britain and Russia, settling in Nice for the winter season. In 1860, Nice voted to reunite with France and entered an era of prosperity. The town's infrastructures were modernised with the extension of the railway and the port, and the construction of new luxurious residential districts and grand hotels, making it the fabulous city and tourist destination we know today.

Map of Nice

Raoul Mille library
Nice-Digne Railway Station
Av. Malausséna
Rue Vernier
Rue Trachel
Boulevard Gambetta
Saint-Nicolas Cathedral
Bd. Tsarévitch
Voie Mathis Voie
Nice railway station
Notre-Dame Basilica
Boulevard Fr. Grosso
Rue Gounod
Rue Rossini
Rue Alphonse Karr
Rue Verdi
Boulevard Victor Hugo
Rue Meyerbeer
Rue du Maréchal Joffre
Rue de la Buffa
Fine Arts Museum
Rue de France
Villa Furtado-Heine
C.U.M.
Negresco
Villa Masséna
Palais de la Méditerranée
Promenade des Anglais
BAIE DES ANGE

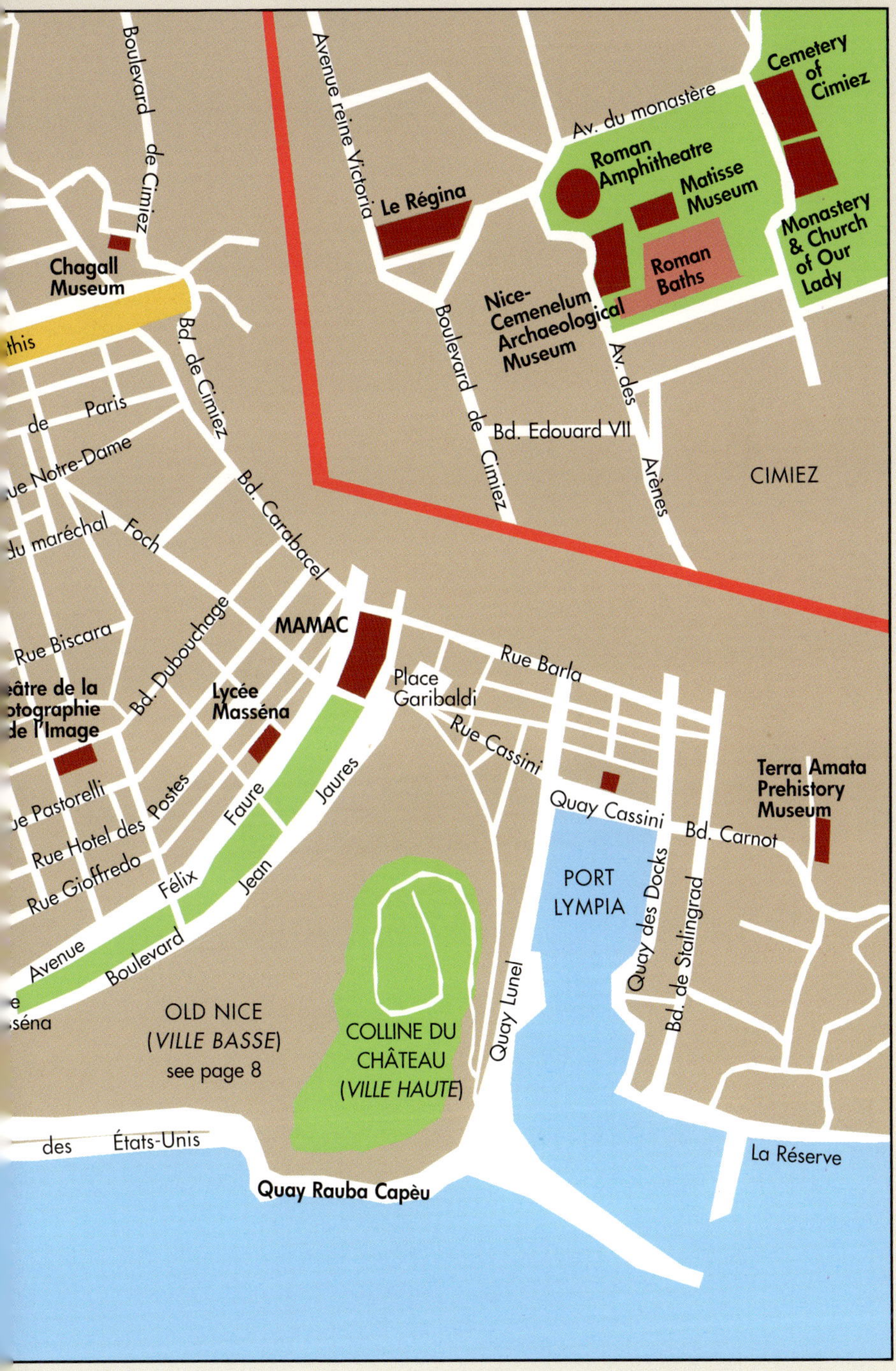
Boulevard de Cimiez
Avenue reine Victoria
Av. du monastère
Cemetery of Cimiez
Roman Amphitheatre
Matisse Museum
Le Régina
Roman Baths
Monastery & Church of Our Lady
Chagall Museum
Nice-Cemenelum Archaeological Museum
Boulevard de Cimiez
Bd. de Cimiez
Av. des Arènes
Bd. Edouard VII
CIMIEZ
Paris
Notre-Dame
maréchal Foch
Bd. Carabacel
Rue Biscara
MAMAC
Bd. Dubouchage
Lycée Masséna
Place Garibaldi
Rue Barla
Rue Cassini
Quay Cassini
Terra Amata Prehistory Museum
Bd. Carnot
Rue Pastorelli
Rue Hotel des Postes
Rue Gioffredo
Félix Faure
Jean Jaures
Avenue
Boulevard
PORT LYMPIA
Quay des Docks
Bd. de Stalingrad
Quay Lunel
OLD NICE (VILLE BASSE) see page 8
COLLINE DU CHÂTEAU (VILLE HAUTE)
des États-Unis
Quay Rauba Capèu
La Réserve

ZOOM IN ON OLD NICE

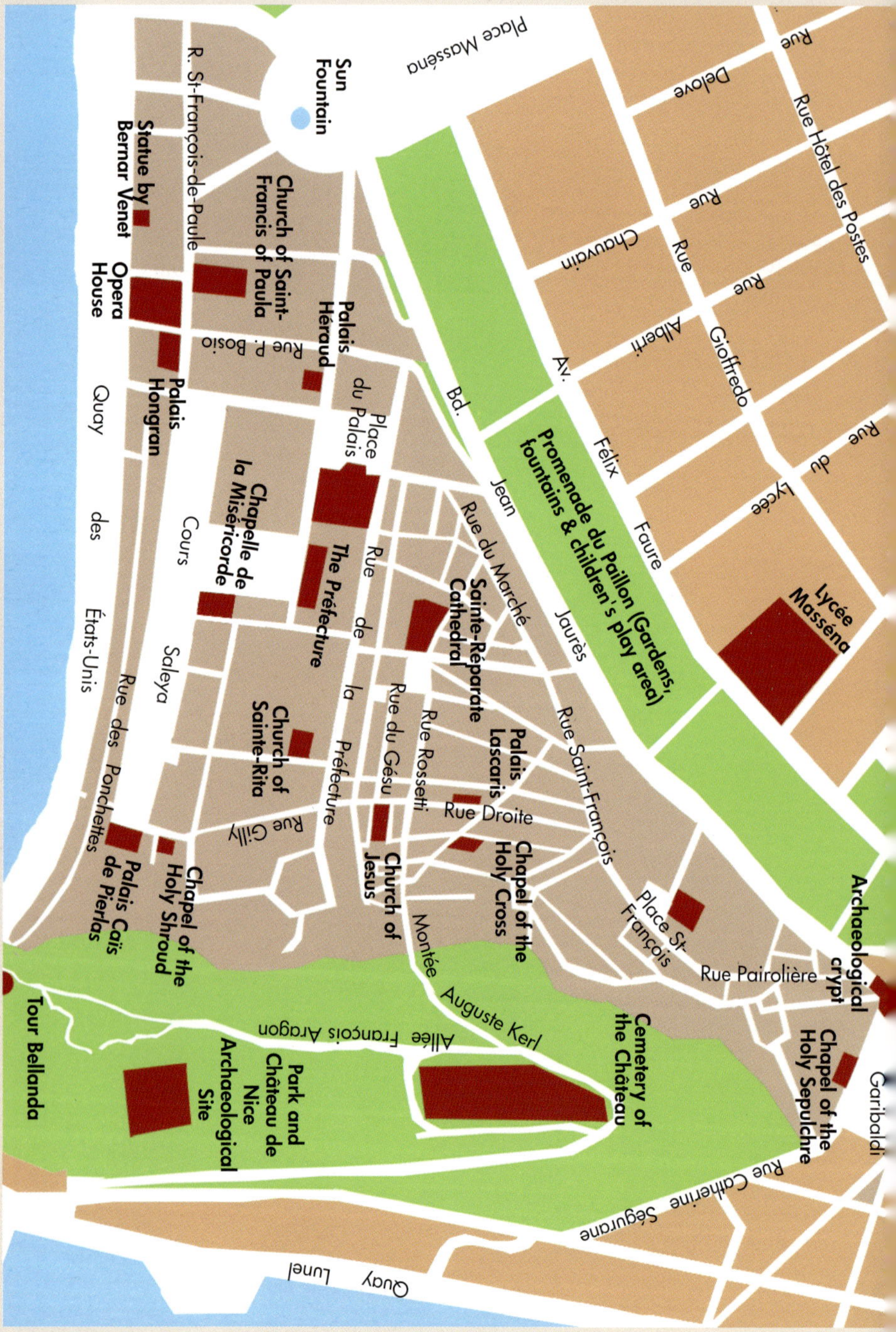

WALKS AROUND NICE

Explore Nice with our Guide's selection of well-documented themed walks and remarkable heritage sites. For quick and easy reference, we have chosen an additional five walking tours around the central districts of Nice (*quartiers*), which offer a diversity of historic and cultural attractions to stop at on the way.

The Old Town (*Vieux-Nice*)

Not to be missed! This walking tour (a leisurely 4 hours) takes you from Place Garibaldi to the site of Nice's former hilltop fort, visiting the following monuments on the way.

The Promenade des Anglais

This tour (2 ½ hours) takes you the length of the "Prom", from the Fine Arts Museum to the Ponchettes Terraces, highlighting some stunning art venues and architectural treasures en route.

From the Port to Garibaldi

On this tour (2 ½ hours), 400,000 year old prehistoric dwellings contrast with the world's first "inhabited sculpture".

Cimiez

Discover a Roman city, the worlds of Matisse and Chagall, and Queen Victoria's love affair with Nice (3 ½ hours).

Town center

Tram and walk across central Nice visiting places of special interest - don't miss the Russian Cathedral (2 ½ hours).

1

THE PROMENADE DES ANGLAIS

THANKS TO THE ENGLISH !

The exotic appeal of the Promenade des Anglais; its palm trees silhouetted against the turquoise blue of the Baie des Anges, was perfectly captured by Raoul Dufy in the 1920's in a collection of thirty paintings, three of which may be seen at the Nice Museum of Fine Arts (see page 99). Redesigned and extended several times since its creation in 1822, the Promenade des Anglais has become the showcase of Nice. Its name refers to the wealthy English tourists who throughout the 19th century spent the winter season here and enjoyed strolling along the seashore, a tradition kept alive by the residents of Nice today.

DISTRICT
Promenade des Anglais - see map page 6

DATES
From the 19th century to the present day

From Wild Shore to the most famous Promenade in the World!

Towards the end of the 18th century, wealthy foreign families took to over-wintering in Nice attracted by its gentle climate and luxuriant natural setting. Promenading along the seafront to take the sea air was prescribed by doctors to strengthen weak constitutions and relieve respiratory disease, endemic at the time. The once popular Ponchettes terrace walkways of the Old Town gradually fell out of favour, too far from the new district across the river that was growing rapidly along the road to France (prior to 1860, Nice was not part of France). In 1822, an Anglican pastor set up a charity to collect funds from his compatriots to build a public walkway for recreation in place of the dirt track that ran along the shore. The Niçois called it "Lou camin dei Anglès".

Le Quai du Midi - Nice in 1862.
Photo by Charles Nègre, Théâtre de la Photographie et de l'Image

INTERVIEW

THE ORIGINS OF THE PROMENADE DES ANGLAIS

Jean-Baptiste Pisano
(Historian)

Jean-Baptiste Pisano, Chair of Art History and Archaeology at the University of Nice.

Can you describe the Promenade des Anglais prior to 1822?

We have two precious sources of records which help us figure out the state of the Promenade prior to 1822. Firstly, the pictorial material available to us. The painting by Jules Defer, for example, now on exhibition at the Villa Massena, which although it dates from a much later period, gives us a view of the seafront at Magnan in 1865 still in its original state. This shows a narrow shore along which a simple road, la route de France, wends its way across the countryside. We also have architectural documentation. The oldest mansion today on the Promenade des Anglais is the Officers Villa also known as the Villa Furtado-Heine. When it was built in the 18th century as a country residence by Lady Penelope Rivers, it was far from the city and the Promenade did not yet exist. This explains why the front of the house looks onto the Route de France and the garden opens out onto the bay.

When was the Promenade des Anglais made suitable for traffic?

Two dates come to mind : 1864 and 1906. Firstly in 1864, the Promenade des Anglais was linked for the first time to the Quai du Midi (now the Quai des Etats-Unis) with the construction of the bridge (le Pont Napoléon or the Pont des Anges) at the mouth of the Paillon river. This is where elegant society gathered to walk in the gardens or go to the first casino built in 1867. During the last part of the century, the construction of big hotels (Anglais, Savoy, Westminster...) on the Promenade went hand in hand with the expansion of the winter tourist season. By 1856 the Promenade reaches Magnan and is already an attractive avenue eight meters wide, but it will be another fifty years before it reaches the hippodrome on the banks of the Var river in 1906.

The Pont Napoléon on the promenade des Anglais, Nice in 1862.
Photo by Charles Nègre, Théâtre de la Photographie et de l'Image

The Promenade des Anglais with the Negresco and the *Palais de la Méditerranée* seen from Rauba Capèu

The French version "la Promenade des Anglais" was adopted in 1844. By 1906, having been progressively widened and elevated above beach level, it now stretched from the banks of the river Var to Rauba Capèu. Between 1920 and 1950, further widening of the road was required with the increase in motor traffic. Growing interest in alternative means of transport is reversing this trend today.

Angels in the Bay

Legends say that the bay was named after the heavenly angels who flew down to rescue shipwrecks or who escorted the body of Réparate, the patron saint of Nice, when her boat festooned with flowers and palm fronds drifted into the bay. Another story tells that Niçois fishermen have always called the bay "mar dei ange" after the huge fish "squatina angelus" which abounded in the sea. This small shark has little fins like angel wings. Local people called the coastal path "camin dei Ange" (Angels' path).

Sea-bathing and the tourist seasons

Tobias Smollett, a Scottish writer and doctor who lived in Nice, praised the virtues of sea-bathing in a series of letters published in 1764. Suffering from lung disease, he discovered the curative benefits of a short daily swim as soon as spring arrived. Intrigued, the Duke of Savoy's palace guards and a number of locals quickly followed suit. Despite the popularity of water therapy since the 18th century, year-round sea-bathing remains even today a practice reserved for a small number of enthusiasts. The winter tourist season at Nice continued to expand with the arrival of the railway in 1864. Big hotels and casinos were built on the Promenade during the Belle Epoque, the first of which was the Hôtel Victoria (West End) in 1858, followed by the Royal Hôtel (1905), the Negresco (1913) (see p. 14) and the Palais de la Méditérranée (1929) (see p. 18). In August 1936, the first paid holidays for workers were introduced rendering seaside holidays accessible to all, moving the peak holiday season from winter/spring to summer.

The Blue Chairs
Photo by Jean-Louis Martinetti – Nice

The Prom's Blue Chairs

In 1950, Charles Tordo, a train engineer from Tourettes-Levens, and inventor in his free time, was asked to create a new design for the Ballanger chair-hire company on the Prom. Mr Tordo came up with the famous Blue Chair. The first 800 chairs were built entirely after hours by the Tordo family. A painting machine and another device to bend the metal frame into its distinctive form were specially built for their manufacture and beech and plane wood were sourced from local forests. The Blue Chair was such a success that Mr Tordo joined the Ballanger firm making Blue Chairs for over 20 years. The latest version can be found on the Prom between the Negresco and the Ruhl hotels.

Sacha Sosno
One of Nice's foremost Artists

Sacha Sosno (1937-2013), sculptor and creator of *La Tête Carrée* (see page 86), held that "the best gallery for sculpture is the street, the beach, a square...". A splendid example of his work can be seen on the façade of the Hôtel Marriott, 57 Promenade des Anglais. Marrying sculpture and architecture, a giant bronze classical Venus emerges, with stunning effect, from between two starkly massive granite walls. Sosno lived as a boy at the Regina and was inspired to paint by Matisse. A remarkable man and gifted artist, Sosno also worked as a war reporter and photographer and crossed the Atlantic Ocean in a yacht. After travelling and exhibiting the world over from India, to Japan and Greece, he returned to Nice to set up his studio amongst the olive groves and vineyards of Bellet.

HOW TO GET THERE

The start of the walk can be reached by bus : N° 8, 11, 52, 59, 60, 62, 70 – Bus stop : Gambetta – Promenade.

WHAT TO SEE

A pleasant one hour walk along the Promenade will take you past a number of monuments and sites which have become iconic attractions of Nice. The walk begins in front of the Negresco at N° 37 Promenade des Anglais and takes you to the Quai Rauba Capèu, past the Villa Masséna (N° 35 – see page 99), the West End Hotel (N° 31), the Royal Hotel (N° 23), the Palais de la Méditérrannée (N° 13 – see page 18), the Jardin Albert 1er public garden, then on to the Quai des États-Unis : the Opera of Nice (see page 85), the Ponchettes (see pages 27 and 89 – The Ponchettes Gallery (N° 77) and the Heritage Centre (N° 75) and Rauba Capèu (see page 34).

2

THE NEGRESCO

MUCH MORE THAN A HOTEL

On the Promenade des Anglais stands one of the world's greatest hotels : the Negresco. This palace hotel with its pristine neo-classical white facade, baroque ornamentation and dusty pink dome is the perfect illustration of the splendour of Nice in the early 20th century. The epitome of French luxury; the Negresco's collection of art and antiques displayed throughout the hotel is worthy of a museum. The hotel owes its unique quality to two long periods of private ownership; owners who had vision and foresight.

WHAT TO SEE
The hotel and its interior decorations

DISTRICT
Promenade des Anglais - see map page 6

DATES
1913 to the present day

Henri Negresco's Dream come True

Henri Negresco was born in Bucarest in 1868. The son of an innkeeper, he left Romania at the age of 15 to travel across Europe, playing the gypsy violin and acquiring a number of languages on the way. His long career in the hotel business began as a clerk, moving up the ranks in the leading hotels of a number of European capitals to become, thanks to his good looks, intelligence and elegantly courteous manner, the indispensable *Maître d'* to an immensely wealthy international clientele. In 1910, he decided to try his luck on the Côte d'Azur where the European elite he had rubbed shoulders with came to enjoy the mild winters. *Maître d'hôtel* at the Monegasque Hôtel Du Helder, then director of the restaurant at the Casino Municipal de Nice, recently renovated by architect Edouard Niermans; Henri Negresco was by then

The Negresco opened its doors in 1913

INTERVIEW
A SHOWCASE FOR FRENCH ART

Jeanne Augier
(Owner of the Hôtel Negresco)

Madame Augier is the owner and CEO of the Negresco since 1957.

How do you remember the hotel before you acquired it?
I thought of it like everyone else in Nice as "The" Palace. At the time, it was compared to Nice's other grand hotel, The Ruhl, but I have to admit that before buying the Negresco, I did visit the Ruhl and realised that I could acquire the Negresco and transform it much more easily than I could have the Ruhl. That was one of the reasons for our initial decision. In my opinion, it was better built and given that I was formerly in the building business with my parents, I was well placed to judge.

How did you go about preserving the Negresco's prestigious reputation and ensuring that it flourished?
My fervent wish was that the Negresco should not be one of those impersonal international palace hotels that are completely soulless. For 50 years now, I have been continually renovating and updating the hotel, adapting to the lifestyle of each era and I especially make a point of keeping up with the latest technologies. I love my country and through French Art I want to make our foreign guests' stay so memorable that they long to return. That is why my collection is made up of genuine period pieces – furniture, pictures, sculptures – and why I also buy contemporary works. I wanted the Negresco's decor to set it apart from the other hotels. When I arrived here, I was staggered to find that all the French palace hotels used the same carpeting and that there was a choice of exactly three colours for fabric wall hangings. I couldn't accept anything so monotonous for my Negresco; my child, in which I could bring my ideas to life, so I had carpets specially created for the hotel in contemporary colours and inspired by the different historic periods of France. People travel to get away and see new things. Our rôle is to help our guests do just that by offering gracious hospitality and a change of scenery.

Salon royal - **Crédit Négresco**

The Negresco

dreaming of building a new palace hotel on a site adjacent to the Villa Masséna on the Promenade des Anglais. He succeeded in persuading the automobile constructor Alexandre Darracq to finance his project and entrusted the plans to Niermans. The engineer Gustave Eiffel, famous for the Eiffel Tower in Paris, was asked to build the dome.

A Modern Palace Hotel with its Own Unique Style

The inauguration on 4 January 1913 of the Côte d'Azur's biggest palace hotel was a memorable event attended by seven reigning sovereigns. It was an immediate success with profits of 800,000 gold francs for its first year of operation! Guests were bedazzled by the Royal Salon with its Louis XVI decor and unusual elliptic form, the sunny rotunda and the specially commissioned outsize carpet, and the luxurious furnishings designed by Paul Dumas for each of the 450 rooms. The Negresco was, in 1913, a pioneer of modernity with all the latest technical innovations : electric commutators, a suction air-cleaning system throughout the hotel, a steam autoclave, telephones and mail delivered directly by tube into each guestroom. Built on the eve of the First World War at the height of the Belle Epoque, the hotel was a favourite of the Russian Grand Dukes. Sadly, the events over the next four years shattered the dreams of the enterprising Romanian. By the time the war was over, the rich clientele had long fled the Côte d'Azur and the glittering new hotel which had been requisitioned as a military hospital, had suffered badly. The long and complex compensation claim procedures to repair the extensive damage finally left

Henri Negresco bankrupt. He died penniless in Paris at the age of 52. The hotel was taken over by the Belgian Marquet group and once again, the world's rich and famous flocked to the Negresco until the Second World War rudely interrupted its newfound prosperity. At the end of the hostilities, the hotel was a mere shadow of itself.

New Beginnings with the Augier Era

Jeanne Augier's family became proprietors of the Negresco in the mid 1950's by a quirk of fate. Her mother, a wealthy property developer, found herself confined through a sudden loss of mobility to her apartment on the Promenade des Anglais. "In all Nice, only the Negresco had lifts wide enough for a wheelchair. We heard that it was for sale, so we bought it." Jeanne Augier and her husband took over a business that, in 1957, was floundering. Staff uniforms were in disrepair for lack of funds and the hotel employed only 76 staff (260 today). Mindful of France's unique cultural heritage, the couple dearly wanted their hotel to become a jewel case for French Art. Over the years, they put together an eclectic collection of antiques and classical and modern art with which they decorated the hotel : priceless pieces of furniture, decorative objects and royal portraits are displayed alongside contemporary works by Moretti, Sosno and Niki de Saint Phalle. The culinary arts are intrinsic to French cultural heritage and the hotel's gastronomic restaurant is Michelin-starred. Paul Augier passed away in 1995. His widow continues to live on the top floor of her hotel; a hotel she has transformed into a veritable museum for her guests to enjoy and share her love of Art. She is the last independent owner of a world-class hotel on the Riviera, resisting bids from the big hotel groups and wealthy investors. The Negresco which was listed as an historic monument in 1974, continues to draw the stars of the film, cultural and artistic worlds as well as heads of state and royalty. In 2010, the hotel underwent its most comprehensive and costly renovation yet with the creation on the 5th floor of a privately accessed "executive floor " equipped with cutting-edge technology. 12 months of lavish celebrations marked the Negresco's 100th anniversary from July 2012 to June 2013 : a truly exceptional hotel.

Neo-classical architecture

HOW TO GET THERE

Address : 13-15 Promenade des Anglais. Tel : 04 93 16 64 00

Bus : 3, 9, 10, 22, 23 – Bus stop : Gambetta – Dante

Bus : 8, 11, 52, 59, 60, 62, 70 – Bus stop : Gambetta – Promenade

From the airport – Bus 98 – Bus stop : Gambetta – Promenade

WHAT TO SEE

Admire the many works of art exhibited on the terrace and inside the hotel, the interior decorations, and liveried doormen. Drop by for cocktails and jazz at the bar. Don't miss a visit to the exceptional Villa Massena, next to the Negresco, at N° 35, Promenade des Anglais (see page 99) – cross the Rue de Rivoli for access via the gardens.

3

THE PALAIS DE LA MÉDITERRANÉE

GRANDEUR AND DECADENCE

This building must have generated the most press articles in all of Nice from its very beginnings to the sordid events of the Agnes Le Roux affair which finally led to its closure towards the end of the 1970's. The Palais's heiress disappeared in mysterious circumstances, presumably victim of a murder. However, like the phoenix rising from the ashes, the Palais de la Méditerranée which has retained its superb original Art Deco facades, ranks once again amongst Nice's leading palace hotels.

WHAT TO SEE
The hotel and its Art Deco facades

DISTRICT
Promenade des Anglais
see map page 6

DATES
1929 to the present day

The Roaring Twenties

The mild winter climate of the Côte d'Azur and the new palace hotels with their panoramic views across the Baie des Anges drew a wealthy clientele to Nice again after the First World War. This was the Roaring Twenties (see page 80) when pleasure seeking reigned and sea-bathing and casinos were all the rage. At the time, Nice already had two major entertainment establishments : the Pier (*la Jetée-Promenade*) and the Municipal Casino, but Joseph Aletti, director of several French palace hotels including the Negresco and the Majestic, had a grand ambition : to build the world's most splendid casino. Backed by the American billionaire Frank Jay Gould, together with the municipality and the leading tourist trade associations; the casino, a theatre and a restaurant with tables for 2,000 guests

were inaugurated in January 1929. Designed by the Niçois architects Charles and Marcel Dalmas, the use of reinforced concrete allowed unprecedented heights and volumes. The awe-inspiring facades adorned with feminine figures and seahorses and the exuberant display of luxury of the interior decorations in the new Art Deco style : (monumental crystal chandeliers, bronzes, exotic woods, stately white marble staircase and immense stained-glass windows) attracted many celebrity visitors including the President of the Republic Doumergue, Maurice Chevalier, Edith Piaf, Sacha Guitry... The Palais de la Méditérranée became a rallying point for the aristocracy and the cultural and arts worlds from all over Europe. While the architecture of the exterior is a mix of Art Deco and classical references in the Fine Arts School tradition, greater creative freedom is revealed in the design of the interior and the lighting. The stained-glass windows of the theatre atriums and the baccarat room were designed by the Parisian glass blower Lebouret. After the Second World War, the building was modernised largely losing its Art Deco style.

Feminine figures and seahorses of the Art Deco facade of the Palais de la Méditerranée

A Laborious Rescue Operation

Mismanagement, financial problems and, above all, the Le Roux Affair put the operating company of the Palais into court-ordered liquidation in 1978. Bought out by investors who planned to pull it down, the remaining decorations, furniture and stained-glass windows were sold at auction in 1981. Although the casino itself was entirely demolished in 1990, both Art Deco façades on the Promenade des Anglais and the Rue du Congrès were listed as an historic monument on 18th August 1989 at the initiative of Jack Lang, then Minister of Culture, in respons to the cries of alarm from a number of public figures who had joined forces with several groups of citizens mobilized to prevent its destruction. Today the Palais de la Méditérrannée is a luxury hotel complex with casino, restaurants, solarium and pool run by Hyatt Regency Hotels and Resorts.

HOW TO GET THERE

Address : 13-15 Promenade des Anglais. Tel. : 04 92 14 77 00
Bus : N°. 8, 11, 52, 60, 62 – Bus stop : Massenet
From the airport – Bus 98 – Bus stop : Congrès – Promenade

WHAT TO SEE

Only the Art Deco facades have been preserved. Today the building has been transformed into a casino and luxury hotel complex. Not far along the Promenade, are the renowned *Belle Époque* hotels : The Royal (N° 23), Hôtel West End (N° 31) and The Negresco (N° 37).

4

PLACE MASSÉNA

TWO HUNDRED YEARS OF HISTORY

At the intersection of the city's two main thoroughfares, Place Masséna with its seven statues by the sculptor Jaume Plensa is Nice's vibrant central square. It has two well-defined areas revealing its construction in several stages. To the north, buildings with red ochre façades and arcades enclose a square with checkerboard black and white paving. To the south is the crescent-shaped Place Charles-Albert where the monumental statue of Apollo dedicated to the sun by Alfred Auguste Janniot, towers above the baroque fountain.

WHAT TO SEE
Place Masséna and the Sun Fountain

DISTRICT
Masséna - see map p. 6

DATES
From the 19th century to the present day

From Marshes to the Place Charles-Albert

In the Middle Ages, the right bank of the river Paillon consisted of marshes and farmlands. The city was contained within its defensive walls until their destruction after the victorious siege of Nice in 1705 by Louis XIV. The ensuing peace between France and the Duchy of Savoy created favourable conditions for the extension of the town; initially around the Place Garibaldi and, on the right bank, along the Route de France (parallel to what will later become the Promenade des Anglais). Place Masséna has its beginnings at the western end of the Old Town with the construction of the crescent-shaped square, the Place Charles-Albert. In the neo-classical style, it was completed in 1830 and illustrates a return to sobriety after the extravagances of the Baroque era.

Place Masséna and the Avenue Jean Médecin
Photo by Pierre Behar

INTERVIEW

PLACE MASSÉNA BETWEEN HISTORY AND MODERNITY

Olivier-Henri Sambucchi

(Curator of Cultural Heritage)

Olivier-Henri Sambucchi is Head Curator of Cultural Heritage and Deputy General Director in charge of Culture for the City of Nice.

Would you say that Jaume Plensa's sculptures (see page 22) serve as an interface between this historic square and a city at the forefront of modernity?

The creation of the tramway gave Nice Côte d'Azur a powerful opportunity to commission contemporary artworks for the public domain thereby making a strong statement of modernity regarding the city's future evolution. The present collection of works which is the result of an international competition, has found its place in Nice's urban landscape transforming it into a vast open-air modern art museum.

When works of art are placed in the public space, the challenge is to achieve metamorphosis by taking a new look at the town's existing built heritage with a view to placing new marks in the landscape, marks which in turn shape the future look of the city. Behind this, there is always the desire to send out a strong signal of contemporaneity and in the case in hand, to reconcile the image of the Côte d'Azur with our modern era, moving it out of the 19th century and into the 21st century. This is the purpose of Jaume Plensa's "Conversation at Nice". The pleasantly ordered composition of regal meditating figures in dialogue, mounted on poles 10 meters high, their conversation symbolised by changing colours which illuminate the night sky, introduces into Nice's city centre a presence that is unusual, artistic, aesthetic and philosophical, and enhances the unity and resplendence of Place Masséna as an architectural entity.

The Southside of the Place Masséna, formerly Place Charles-Albert.
Photo by Patrick Kaminski and Isabelle Landragin

The Place Masséna and *Conversation at Nice* by J. Plensa - Photo by François Fernandez

The *Consiglio d'Ornato* and the Charles-Albert Bridge

In 19th century Nice, the river Paillon constituted a major obstacle to the town's development until the decision was made to build a new bridge (*le Pont-Neuf or the Pont Royal Charles-Albert*) linking the recently built square (*la Place Charles-Albert*) and the Old Town to its right bank. For centuries, the sole means of crossing from one bank to the other had been the medieval bridge (*le Pont-Vieux*) adjacent to the town gate (*la Porte Pariolière*) (see Place Garibaldi – page 42). The problem of access between the city and the now rapidly growing new districts around the Croix-de-Marbre and the church Saint Jean-Baptiste led to the adoption, in 1832, of the Town Planning Scheme and the creation of the Planning Committee (*Consiglio d'Ornato*) in charge of conducting and monitoring the renovation of the town and its urbanisation.

1843 : The Vernier Project (a church right in the middle of the Avenue Jean-Médecin)

As can be observed from the various amendments made to the Planning Scheme between 1832 and 1843, the construction of the new bridge (le Pont-Neuf) was the topic of a fair amount of debate. An initial project, abandoned in 1835, provided for the construction on the right bank of a second square symmetrical to the Place Charles-Albert to be accessed by the new bridge. During this period, Nice had miraculously been left untouched by an outbreak of cholera. The city council launched an architectural competition for a church to be built to the north of the new bridge in thanks to Our Lady of the Graces for her protection. The winning design by the architect Vernier showed an imposing church right in the middle of the north side of the square (Place Masséna) enclosed by buildings (precisely at the entrance to the present avenue Jean Médecin). The project was refused by the Planning Committee and twenty years later the church (*l'église du Voeu*) was built, as had been promised, further up river in the Saint Jean-Baptiste district. A plan for the Place Masséna was finally approved in 1843 : a rectangular square traversed by an avenue and bordered by opulent buildings with arcades.

The Renovations of the 21st century : Contemporary Art in a Heritage Setting

During work on the tramway between 2003 and 2007, the city council voted to transform the Place Masséna and the avenue Jean-Médecin into a vast car-free esplanade, a "green avenue" heading towards the sea. Entirely renovated at a cost of 14 million euros by the architect Bruno Fortier, it is a tranquil pedestrian area paved with black and white flagstones and lit by lanterns and candelabras through which the new tramway passes. The square was awarded a distinction by the Town Planning Trophies in April 2008. Today, its historic splendour has a stamp of modernity with Jaume Plensa's "Conversation at Nice", seven 10 meter high pillared statues representing the continents who, through a subtle play of colours symbolizing the language of Peace, are engaged in conversation.

HOW TO GET THERE

Place Masséna is at the beginning of the Avenue Jean-Médecin and can be reached by tram N° 1 or bus : N° 14, 15, 22 - Bus stop : Masséna Guitry - or tramway – tram stop : Masséna.

WHAT TO SEE

Don't miss the statues by Jaume Plensa bearing their message of Peace, breathtakingly beautiful at nightfall, and the larger than life Arch by Vernet (see p. 86) in the newly planted gardens of the Promenade du Paillon, a vast park stretching all the way from Nice's National Theatre to the Promenade des Anglais. Close by is the Old Town with its narrow medieval streets, Baroque churches (see p. 77) and lively markets of the Cours Saleya (see p. 26).

The Jardin Albert Ier Public Gardens in 1895.
Photo by Charles Nègre, Théâtre de la Photographie et de l'Image.

The Promenade du Paillon - **Photo by Patrick Kaminski and Isabelle Landragin**

The Promenade du Paillon

The *Promenade du Paillon*, Nice's new inner city park, which stretches over one kilometer from the Modern Art Museum and National Theatre to the *Promenade des Anglais*, was opened in Autumn 2013. Visitors may not realize that the park is planted on a slab covering a river that divides the city in two. The River Paillon is a typically Mediterranean river that diminishes to a small stream for part of the year (19th century laundry women, *bugadiera*, used to lay their washing out to dry on the river bed) but swelled by sudden rain and melting snow from the Alps can turn into a raging torrent. From the end of the 19th century, it was decided to cover the river, extending the Place Masséna, and facilitating communication between the Old and New Towns.

The new park, designed by the innovative landscape architects, Péna & Péna, offers 30 acres of contemporary gardens, an enchanting mirror of water with fountains, children's' play areas and peaceful walkways, and draws attention to vistas of Nice that have been hidden for many years. Péna & Péna seek to create a green urban space, where town and nature are intimately entwined, carefully selecting plants adapted to the microclimate of Nice, and inventing gardens "full of life where children play in fountains". The delightful play areas are equipped with huge wooden marine-animal climbing frames invented by the French sculptor, David Steinfield. The *Promenade du Paillon* is a model of 21st century sustainable development with the use of eco-friendly materials, programmed lighting (by Yves Adrien), drought resistant plants and water-saving ground cover.

Casa Nissa

ife is beautiful. Thank you for enjoying it

ome to Casa Nissa for an unforgettable gastronomic, ual and musical experience. an authentic Niçois decor, our our Mediterranean sine, featuring dishes from ovence, Spain and Italy, and nes from southern sun-nched vineyards. Take a tour Nice's historic and cultural treasures with our innovative visual displays, join live *Latin canto y baile music* evenings (Thursday to Saturday) and enjoy al sco eating amongst the olive trees on our terrace.

* * * * *

Menus 21.50€ /28€ / 34€ À la carte PM.30€
"Maître Restaurateur" Quality Assurance"
(Traditional home-made cooking using fresh ingredients)
Nice (Place Massena) 55 rue Gioffredo
(Opposite Galeries Lafayette – Masséna car park)
Tél. 04 93 80 30 19 - www.casa-nissa.com

5

THE COURS SALEYA

TAKING TIME OUT TO WATCH THE WORLD GO BY

"All roads lead to Rome; here in the Old Town, they lead to the Cours Saleya", Nice's best loved novelist, the late Louis Nucera liked to say of this historic square with its ochre weather-worn facades, enchanting backdrop of green woods and waterfall cascading down from Castle Hill where an ancient citadel had once stood. Only a few steps from the beaches and the "Med", this is a place to take time out to enjoy the cheery bustle of the markets or linger on a café terrace watching the world go by.

WHAT TO SEE
The markets, baroque chapels (see page 74) and Bellanda Tower

DISTRICT
The Old Town – see map page 8

DATES
From the 18th century to the present day

The cours Saleya (1770)

The name *Saleya* (20th century) possibly refers to the existence of ancient wine cellars. "*Il Palco*", known affectionately as "*Le Cours*", adopted its present form in the late 18th century : an elongated square at the heart of the busy Marine district between the Duke of Savoy's palace gardens and the old port of Nice (see page 36). In place of the city walls, dismantled in 1706, a terrace of warehouses and fishermens' cottages had been built. In 1770, the roof of the terrace was transformed into a public walkway overlooking the tree-lined Cours and the bay to the south. The Ponchettes Terraces (see page 27), together with the lively commerce of cafés and shops, drew the wealthy winter visitors to the Cours. A second walkway, "The New Terraces" was built on the seafront in 1839, becoming, with the Promenade des Anglais (1822) and the Albert Ier public gardens (1852), one of the fashionable meeting places where winter tourists met and strolled together to admire the spectacular seascapes (see photo page 27).

Louis-Gilles Pairault

(Curator)

Louis-Gilles Pairault was Curator of the Heritage of Nice and Director of the Nice Municipal Archives.

How were the Ponchettes Terraces used in the 19th century?

The *Terrasses des Ponchettes*, which had been created in the mid-eighteenth century, was where people congregated to walk. The foreign winter tourists, in particular, enjoyed strolling along the Terraces to watch the fishermen drawing their boats up onto the shore below or mending their nets. In fact, they offered a double panorama : of the beaches and the bay to the south and, to the north, the roofs of the Old Town (where tourists rarely ventured) and the ring of snow capped mountains beyond. Of course, when the Promenade des Anglais was built in 1822, it drew the crowds away from the Terrraces and eventually, over a period of time, supplanted them altogether. Their popularity was still so great towards the end of the 1830's that a new walkway above a second row of terraces, the new (*Terrasses Neuves*) was built along the shore, parallel to the *Terrasses des Ponchettes*.

What would you expect to find on the Cours Saleya in the 19th century?

The Cours was the central hub of society life; it was a shady square where one could go to walk, meet people to chat, eat or have a drink in the sun, (yes, all that already happened!) after having taken a stroll on the Terraces. It was also an important centre of commerce and therefore of working class life too with the shops and markets. At the end of the century, the famous flower market of Nice was formally established on the Cours. As it was close the seat of central power at the Palais Sarde (the Duke's Palace), now the Préfecture of the Alpes-Maritimes, this was where rallies and popular events, political meetings and public ceremonies were held : these included royal visits, the proclamation of the Constitution (Statuto) in 1848, the official ceremony uniting Nice with France, as well as Carnival merrymaking from 1873.

The quai du Midi *(Quai des États-Unis)* and the Ponchettes Terraces – Nice, 1865.
Photo: Charles Nègre – Théâtre de la Photographie et de l'Image.

The Cours Saleya with the Ponchettes Terraces on the right - Photo: Pierre Behar

Stationer to H.M. Queen Victoria

Visconti's Literary Establishment, founded in 1839 was, for over sixty years, one of the great cultural attractions of the Cours Saleya, counting amongst its clients visiting foreign royals and aristocrats, local artists and intellectuals. Open every day from 8 a.m. to 10.30 p.m., it was a bookshop, international lending library and newsagents, stationery and art shop, smoking, reading and conversation rooms, and art gallery all rolled into one. Visconti's also edited a newspaper, published books and hired rooms for conferences, exhibitions and charity events. Their terrace was THE place in town to hold a reception, and an ideal vantage point from which to view the Carnival merrymaking. Visconti's is no longer there, but the original shop of another traditional family business is. The Librairie Rontani, opened in 1907 at 5, rue Alexandre Mari, continues to display the mention "*By appointment Stationer to* H.M. *Queen Victoria*", and provide a good selection of cards, art materials, travel guides and maps.

Cours Saleya Markets

After 1860, the town's wholesale, flower and farmers' markets were centralized on the Cours Saleya. For over a century, however, the fruit and vegetable market continued to join the booksellers (bouquinists) at the Winter Market on the banks of the Paillon River (which was not covered over at the time), returning to the Cours Saleya in summertime. Strict regulations have been applied since the Middle Ages to street trading licences, specified pitches, opening hours (during which time a market flag was flown) and the quality of produce sold at Nice's markets.

Today, markets are held all year round on the Cours Saleya (see WHAT TO SEE).

Market porters and the small trades

Market porters were employed by the wholesalers and stall-holders. They belonged to a guild and wore a "jijoula", a copper medal bearing their employer's name. They set up and dismantled the stalls, made deliveries on a small cart or acted as vendors and cashiers. The "portefaix" carried goods on their heads in baskets made of strips of chestnut wood. One of the colourful characters on the Cours towards the end of the 19th century, "La Matouna", had a successful business renting benches to the stallholders for the princely sum of 2 centimes. No market would have been complete without its sellers of pissaladière and socca, still favourite Niçois "slow-foods" today (see page 109).

The Tour Bellanda

The Tour Bellanda, an imposing round tower, was built in 1825 by Mr Clérissi on the site of a ruined medieval tower, the Tour Saint-Elme, once part of the massive ramparts of the fortress of Nice. It later became an annexe to the Clérissi boarding house next door (now the Hôtel Suisse). The 17th century historian, Honoré Bouche, claimed that the castle on the hill was known in the Middle Ages as the "Tour Bellanda" ("beautiful land" in Latin). The Tour Bellanda has had a colourful history. From 1536 - 1543, the Holy Shroud of Turin was brought to Nice for safekeeping by the exiled Duke of Savoy, Charles III. It had been in his family's possession since 1453. On Good Friday 1537, the Duke gave permission to the Bishop of Nice to display the Shroud from the top of the Tour Saint-Elme for the veneration of the faithful and to entreat heavenly protection against the calamities which had hit the region. The tower is also famed as the place where, in 1844, Berlioz "set up quarters" and was inspired to compose his intensely original work *La Tour de Nice*, later reworked to become *The Corsair*. On a previous idyllic stay in 1831 at the Clérissi boarding house, he had written the "*King Lear*" overture "That is how I spent the three most superb weeks of my life in Nice. O Nizza!" He would return once again to Nice in 1868.

The Bellanda Tower

HOW TO GET THERE

Tramway N° 1 : tram stop : Opera-Vieille Ville, Cathédrale - Vieille Ville. Bus: N° T32 - Bus stop : Cours Saleya

WHAT TO SEE

The markets on the Cours Saleya :

- Flea Market – Monday from 6 a.m. to 5 p.m.
- Flower Market – Tuesday to Saturday from 6 a.m. to 5 p.m. Sunday from 6 a.m. to 12.30 p.m.
- Fruit, Vegetable and Farmers Market - Tuesday to Sunday 7 a.m. to 1 p.m

The Baroque Chapels :
The Chapelle de la Miséricorde, 7 cours Saleya (open on Tuesday afternoon) and the Chapelle du Saint-Suaire (see page 79).

The Baroque Mansions (Palazzi) :
The Palais Caïs de Pierla, 1 place Charles-Félix and the Palais Hongran, 2 rue Saint-François-de-Paule. (see page 76).

The Tour Bellanda : Montée Lesage (between Rauba Capèu and Rue des Ponchettes). Closed to the public.

6

THE CHÂTEAU

THE COLLINE DU CHÂTEAU AND ITS MEDIEVAL RUINS

From the Middle Ages, Nice was caught in a tug-of-war between France and Italy. Coveted by Genova, in the 12th century, and by Louis XIV, King of France, five hundred years later, to the point of becoming a veritable obsession, Nice has always held a key strategic position. The first semblance of a castle (*château*) was perhaps built in or around the 1100's. By the 17th century, successive innnovations and improvements had transformed it into one of the most powerful fortresses in Europe. That is, until Louis XIV decided differently...

WHAT TO SEE
The archaeological dig, the park, the views

DISTRICT
The *Colline du Château*

DATE
From the 5th century to the present day

Significant Dates in the Construction of the Fortress of Nice (*Château*)

Henri Geist, President of the History and Archeological Circle of the Alpes-Maritimes, describes the construction of the fort and significant events that marked its history: "Sometime after the 11th century, a castle protected by a great wall was built on the hilltop (*Colline du Château*). During the same period dwellings appeared on the plateau around the castle and to the north, together with a series of enclosures. During the 15th century, the castle was fortified by a long wall encircling the entire hill. A century later, the complex was reinforced by Charles II of Savoy and housing developed at the foot of the castle. From 1560, a citadel was founded to the north (on the present site of the cemetery – see page 104). At the beginning of the 17th century, the fortifications

View of the Castle from the Old Town at the end of the Middle Ages - **Credit: Archives of the City of Nice**

INTERVIEW

THE *COLLINE DU CHÂTEAU* FROM THE 5TH TO THE 21ST CENTURY

Marc Bouiron

(Archaeologist)

Marc Bouiron is Curator of Cultural Heritage and Director of the Archaeology Service of the City of Nice. Since 2006, he has directed the excavation campaigns and research on the hilltop site (*Colline du Château*) and the castle (*Château*).

When was the first cathedral of Nice built?

Whilst excavating the site of the cathedral which dates back to the 11th century, we uncovered evidence of the existence of an earlier building. Ceramics found in the earth around the foundations date back to the 5th century. The ground plan that emerged (we have been able to identify the external walls) is that of a paleo-christian church which was destroyed when the medieval church was built. We have here the remains of Nice's first cathedral.

Why does so little remain of the *Château* today?

It is true that visitors to the park see few visible traces of the Château, and yet they do exist! Louis XIV's engineers did a thorough job demolishing the fortress with mines. Over the following centuries, the demand for stone to build roads, the Port Lympia of Nice and even the church on the Port finished the work. On top of that, the hill itself served as a quarry, which changed its physiognomy, with, for example, the construction of the War Memorial (see page 37). The creation of the park in the 19th century and the afforestation of the hill completed the dissolution of the fortress. The work we are doing today consists of retracing history in order to reproduce, as precisely as possible, the image of this exceptional heritage site.

Remains of Nice's first cathedral (dating from the 5th century) can be seen in the park on the hill (the *Colline du Château*).

Nice's hilltop fortress town at the end of the 17th century, just prior to its destruction
Painting by Jean-Luc Sauvaigo. Credit: Archives of the City of Nice

were extended and strengthened further and, in 1690, Victor-Amadée II of Savoy modernized the 16th century ramparts. The castle, surrounded by a wall 2.3 kilometers long, was considered invincible."

An Invincible Fortress

In the 17th century, the castle of Nice was considered one of the most powerful in Europe. Contemporary witnesses judged it to be unconquerable. By then, it was a formidable fortress which, together with the ramparts and bastions that encircled the Old Town (*Ville Basse*), was well equipped to defend the town. Nice's defences were not confined to the castle, the citadel and the *Ville Basse* since the county (*comté de Nice*) also had a fortified line of defence stretching from the citadel of Saint-Elme at Villefranche to Nice via the forts of Saint-Hospice at Cap-Ferrat and Montalban. The Montalban fort was built in 1560 on the orders of Emmanuel-Philibert, Duke of Savoy, on the hill dominating the plain of Lympia. The rôle of this small, almost discreet, fort was to control the access between Villefranche and Nice. The citadel Saint-Elme, also built under Emmanuel-Philibert in the 16th century, stood guard over the harbour and protected Nice's military port established at Villefranche. The fort of Saint-Hospice, located on the rocky promontary of the same name adjacent to Cap-Ferrat, defended the coast in direct link with the citadel of Villefranche. After the failed siege in 1543 by the Franco-Turkish alliance, these various defensive structures gave Nice the reputation of being indomitable, which is why, in 1705, it was not expected that Louis XIV would wipe out the entire line of defence.

The Fall of the *Château de Nice*

Louis XIV laid siege to the city of Nice twice during the 17th and 18th centuries with the clear objective to annex the county (*comté de* Nice) and its citadel to France. The first siege took place in 1691: on 12th March, the King's troops, under the command of Monsieur Catinat, invaded Villefranche arriving from the Var and skirting around Nice through the back country. The citadel of Saint-Elme surrendered fairly quickly. On 25th March, Montalban Fort was attacked and did not resist for long. Two days later the army advanced on Nice and its castle. The town (*Ville Basse*) was caught in the crossfire when the castle retaliated to attacks from the trenches built by the invader. At the same time, the French canons continued to bombard the castle until, finally, one of the canonballs struck the great keep containing the powder store causing a tremendous explosion and killing hundreds. The next day, the *Château* capitulated and the French slowly but surely took possession of the whole county. Some three years later, on 24th August 1694, Louis XIV signed the Turin Peace Treaty by which he returned his conquests to Victor-Amadée II, who set to repairing the castle. The second and final siege of Nice took place in 1705 and lasted into 1706. Again the French regiments advanced on Nice from the Var in order to take the town. The troops split into two. Part of the army kept watch over Nice and Villefranche, the other half marched on Sospel and Tende where they blockaded the defence lines and the Royal Route to the Piedmont and the capital, Turin. Sospel fell on 10th March 1705. Nice was taken in two phases: the town surrendered on 5th April 1705, whilst the *Château* continued to resist the bombardments until 4th January 1706. Louis XIV promptly gave orders to destroy the fortifications of Nice and the *Château*. Only Fort Montalban was saved.

A piece of fallen masonry from the fortress (it is lying on its side). It can be seen next to the archaeological site of the cathedral.

HOW TO GET THERE

The *Colline du Château* is freely accessed on foot. To get there, take the steps to the left of the Hôtel Suisse, quai des États-Unis which go up to the Tour Bellanda and the park on the hill. There are also free lift facilities to the left of the steps at the foot of the tower.

Bus: N°. T32 - Bus stop : Cours Saleya :
Bus: N°. 3,7,9,10,14,20,27,30,81,82 -
Bus stop : Le Port

WHAT TO SEE

The views from the park are breathtaking : over the Port or the Baie des Anges as far as Antibes and Cannes, with the mountains of the Var and the foothills of the Alpes in the distance. Make sure you see the archaeological dig of the fortress with its ramparts and the ancient cathedral (N.B. The great keep was at the very summit of the hill (where the souvenir shop is now). The cemetery is worth a visit (see page 104).

7

THE QUAY RAUBA CAPÈU

AND THE WAR MEMORIAL

In Antiquity, the Phoceans came from *Massilia* (Marseille) to Nice to set up a trading post on the hill (*Colline du Château*). Watch was kept from the steep cliff rising up over the bay where the Greek vessels took up moorings. Over the next few hundred years, the town grew and flourished. The destruction of the castle in 1706 and the construction of the present port after 1749, led to the appearance of new structures on the coast such as the Quay Rauba Capèu with its exceptional panorama across the Baie des Anges, and the imposing War Memorial.

WHAT TO SEE
The esplanade, the sundial, the War Memorial

DISTRICT
The Port – see map p. 6

DATES
From the 18th century to the present day

The Quay Rauba Capèu over the centuries

Rauba Capèu, "the hat thief" in Niçois, is a vivid description of what happens when the strong *levante* (east) and *lebech* (south-west) winds clash on this rocky promontory. In 1770, a narrow path was carved out of the rock on the site of the colossal 14th century ramparts (destroyed in 1706). Its purpose was to link the new Port Lympia, which quickly rendered the old Port Saint-Lambert obsolete (see page 38), and access into the Old Town by the *Porte de la Marine*. The *Chemin des Ponchettes* takes its name from pounchetta, little rocky points that project into the sea at the foot of the *Colline du Château*. The path was widened in 1826 for a royal visit by the popular King Charles-Félix and his wife Marie-Christine. The Rauba Capèu terrace has been redesigned several times. A military battery occupied the site until the end of the 19th century when

Quay Rauba Capèu at the foot of the Colline du Château :
Photo by Pierre Behar

Thierry Ciccione
(Architect)

Thierry Ciccione of StoA Architecture Associates, Marseille , is one of the architects who participated in the project to modernise the Quai Rauba Capèu.

How did you modernise Rauba Capèu?
Rauba Capèu is a balcony 300 meters long that was cut out of the rock between the castle and the sea. It stands out in the urban landscape, it does not ressemble at all what one would normally expect to find on a seafront. Beaches, buildings, tree-lined promenades, avenues leading down to the sea come to an abrupt halt at Rauba Capèu. Whereas the Promenade des Anglais and the Quay des Etats-Unis follow the alluvial plain, which is naturally concave, the Quay Rauba Capèu skirts round the rock, which is naturally convex. Elsewhere, the Promenade is kept at a distance from the hills by the town, and from the sea by the beach. Here the Quay is a thin ribbon that threads its way round the headland between the rock and the sea. In other places, the rollers fall gently onto the sand. Here, they crash against the rocks. Elsewhere, views are restricted within a natural frame. Here the full panorama is laid out before us, unhindered, to achieve our respect for the harmony that exists between the various elements.

What is it in your project that made it different?
Toning down the frontal relationship between the land and the sea wasn't an option. We made the choice to highlight the strength of the line in the design. Not a single tree, flagpole, railing, parapet or planter would obstruct the horizon from the view of the passerby. The art of planning public space is simple. The fact that means are limited, for earthworks, surface covering, furniture and planting, requires that particular care is taken to put what is already present on the site to its best advantage. In this case, the panoramic view is enhanced by simply lowering the guardrail. The white stone that had been carved from the hillside where the War Memorial is now located, was the inspiration for the blocks of beautiful hewn limestone.

The sundial on the Quay Rauba Capèu

Rauba Capèu

it was turned over by the army to the city and demolished.

Rauba Capèu Reinvented

Rauba Capèu has a horizontal sundial (1981) which is designed so that the user, by standing on a specific spot, projects a shadow onto the hour lines drawn on the ground thereby indicating the time. In 2003, the entire esplanade was redesigned. The City of Nice asked architects, Thierry Ciccione, Charles Bové and Pascal Urbain, to design a project that would be exemplary, centred on the extension of the cycle path that runs the length of the Promenade des Anglais. The walkway is set at a lower level. It is separated from the pavement by a long stone bench that espouses the generous curves of the esplanade and is protected from the sheer drop below by a guard-rail that is at the same height as the bench. When darkness falls, it is lit by spotlights, becoming a shining trail that winds it way between the rock and the waters below. The project uses all the existing elements: the landscape and the limestone, which echoes the white stone quarried from the *Colline du Château* with which the quays on the Port were built. Nothing halts the eye nor distracts it away from the seascape. The view across the bay at Nice is riveting, but the buildings on the other side of the road with their harmoniously coloured facades are also worthy of attention. Opposite the War Memorial, divers will chance upon the huge statute of the Virgin, Notre-Dame des Fonds Farins, by the sculptor Alfred

Gualiterotti, submerged 15 meters below sea-level. Commissioned by the municipality of Nice, Rauba Capèu's Virgin was blessed on 20 October 1968 by Monseigneur Mouisset, Bishop of the Diocese of Nice, and then lowered into the water by divers and the town fire-fighters.

The War Memorial: The Heavy Price Paid by Nice during the War

The War Memorial is located at the far end of the Quay Rauba Capèu below the Colline du Château in the old quarries that , in the 18th century, supplied the stone for the construction of the wharfs of Port Lympia and, in the 19th century, the Pier on the Promenade. The Memorial, which commemorates the 4,000 Niçois who died for France during the Great War, was built between 1924 – 28. It was designed in the Art Deco Style by the Niçois, Roger Séassal, First Rome Grand Prix in 1913, and Member of the French Academy of Fine Arts who was also the architect of the Casino at Menton, the Nice Science and Law Faculty and the CUM (*Carrefour Universitaire Méditerranéen*). The sculptor Alfred Janniot, Rome Grand Prix in 1929, who also designed the Sun Fountain on the Place Masséna (see page 20) designed the high reliefs.

This awe-inspiring Memorial, which was inaugurated by the Maréchal Foch on 29 January 1929. An urn supported by columns sheltered by three great arches contains a sealed reliquary within which the families placed the identity nameplates of their deceased during the ceremony. High reliefs decorate the pedestal of the urn symbolizing War: Liberty, Strength, the Sacred Fire and Victory on one side and Peace on the other: Work, Love of the Home and Fertility. In 1947, a huge Cross of Lorraine was erected in the middle of a garden of exotic plants to honour the memory of the French Resistance. Also inscribed on the Memorial are the names of soldiers, victims of the Second World War, the War in Indochina and Algeria.

The War Memorial

HOW TO GET THERE

Bus: N° T32 - Bus stop : Tour Bellanda

Bus: N° 3,7,9,10,14,20,27,30,81,82 - Bus stop : Le Port

WHAT TO SEE

Don't miss the Quay Rauba Capèu, its sundial and the monumental War Memorial. If the Quay offers a superb view of the coastline of Nice, it is well worth visiting the neighbouring sights and attractions: The Port – the Tour Bellanda – the *Colline du Château* – the baroque monuments of the Old-Town.

8

LYMPIA
THE PORT

FROM THE PONCHETTES TO PORT LYMPIA

For several hundred years, goods entering Nice by ship were unloaded either directly onto the strand (now the Quai des États-Unis) in front of The Old Town or via the port at Villefranche and then transferred to Nice by horse and cart. New advances in engineering techniques during the 18th century gave the impetus, in 1749, to launch a grand project : to build a port in the Lympia plain, a marshy area to the east of Castle Hill. The construction would only be fully completed under Napoléon III after Nice's reunification with France in 1860.

WHAT TO SEE
The quays and the church Notre-Dame-du-Port

DISTRICT
The Port – see map p. 6

DATES
From the 18th century to the present day

The Ponchettes : An Ancient Greek Fishermens' Port

The older generation of Niçois still remember fishermen in the 1950's pulling their boats up onto the shore at The Ponchettes to sort through their catch and dry their nets; a ritual dating back for 2,000 years, since it was here in this little bay at the foot of Castle Hill that the Greek founders of Nikaïa (Nice) moored their craft. In the 13th century, the port of Saint-Lambert boasted an arsenal, a salt tax office and a fish market and removable pontoons were installed to be used as landing docks. Although the town made a number of attempts throughout the 17th century to modernise the port, this small harbour remained a *marina* (the niçois word for a strand on which all types of ships landed), which lacked facilities such as dikes, wharfs or a lighthouse. The harbour at Villefranche served as Nice's main port for several centuries as it was naturally sheltered from bad weather and was deeper and therefore easier to develop.

The Ponchettes in 1865, Photo by Charles Nègre, Théâtre de la Photographie et de l'Image

INTERVIEW

THE PORT OF NICE IN THE 18TH AND 19TH CENTURIES

Alain Ruggiero

(Historian)

Alain Ruggiero, Specialist in Contemporary History at the University of Nice.

Although it is on the coast, Nice does not have a natural harbour. Can you tell us how the port was built ?

Port Lympia was built on a low budget as Nice was a small state with limited means; the site was a swamp so it was not difficult to dig out and stone blocks were available from the nearby quarry on the hill and also the old fortress which was dismantled in 1706. The harbour facilities as they appear in 18th century prints are very rudimentary; there are no wharfs as such, but at least vessels could take shelter and goods could easily be loaded and unloaded. The port probably also had military objectives, which French observers unremittingly pointed out in their reports. The creation of Port Lympia, together with franchises (tax exemptions) on imported goods stimulated Nice's commercial growth. The "right to asylum" was granted freely to foreign merchants and sailors, many of whom came from Provence, Liguria and Livorno, settling in Nice. This continued right up to the European economic crisis in 1787-1790.

How did the franchises function ?

Although the franchises had been introduced long before, they did not initially have a great impact until after Port Lympia was built, and then again during a second period from 1820 - 1850 when Marseille's requirements for olive oil provided an outlet to the Italian surplus. At the time, the tax exemptions concerned goods entering Nice (not yet part of France). On arrival at Lympia, cargoes were transhipped to vessels flying the French flag, which then sailed on to Marseille. Although in time the franchise system became obsolete, the Niçois were very attached to these privileges and there was some commotion when they came to an end, which undoubtedly contributed in no small way to the people turning away from the House of Savoy, and played a role in the outcome of the referendum to join France in April 1860.

Port Lympia towards 1860
Painting by Hercule Trachel – Museum of Fine Art, Nice

Port Lympia

The Free Port at Villefranche

Olivula Portus, the old Roman port at Villefranche still served as a harbour, in the Middle Ages, for the hilltop castrum, Montolivio, where the inhabitants had taken refuge from the devastating invasions recurrent at that time. In 1295, the Count of Provence founded Villa Franca by fortifying this small but strategic port and granting tax exemptions to encourage the population to reinhabit the coast. In 1388, Villefranche and the county of Nice passed into the House of Savoy. In 1550, after the Port of Villefranche had been taken and occupied by the fleet of the Franco-Ottoman alliance during the siege of Nice, it was restored to the Duke of Savoy, acquiring a new status as port to the duchy's capital, Turin, and home to the Savoyard armada. As Turin's sole access to the sea until 1749 when Port Lympia was founded at Nice, Villefranche was continually upgraded well into the 18th century. Its defences were reinforced, the mole was extended and a lighthouse built, as well as the only dry docks between Genova and Toulon specialised in galley building and maintenance.

The constuction of Port Lympia : an Affair of State

In 1749, the King of Savoy, Charles-Emmanuel III, decided to build a port at Nice which was currently enjoying a period of peace and prosperity. The Lympia site was chosen as Villefranche was lacking building space for warehouses and had taken on an essentially military role. The plan was highly ambitious: to build a large dike and two basins using stone from the fortified town of Nice that Louis XIV had demolished, together with an arms depot, wharfs, warehouses and workshops. The hitherto rural district around the port would also see the development of a whole new commercial, trade and residential quarter. The costs and technical difficulties encountered were such that despite the engineers' prowess and the construction of facilities to improve the efficiency of port activities, the project would only reach completion after Nice had joined France and could benefit from its economic might and technical expertise. Today, the Port of Nice continues to operate in three main domains : commerce, recreational boating and cruises, and links with Corsica.

Niçois fishing boats in the Port at Nice

Round and about the Port : a New District

The construction of a new port at Nice led to the creation of roads and a whole new district. In 1770 – 72, the rocky spur to the south of Castle Hill was levelled to link the two ports by road, the *Chemin des Ponchettes* (*Quai Rauba Capèu*). The Route Royale (the Royal Salt Road) connecting Turin to Nice and Villefranche, which was made suitable for carriages in 1780, arrived at Nice by the Turin Gate at the entrance to the new square, Place Garibaldi (1750 – 80). The Rue du Port (*Rue Ségurane*), built between 1770 – 1790, attracted businesses, entrepots, kitchens and manufacturers associated with the activities of the port. Place Cassini (*Place Île-de-Beauté*) was built between 1820 – 50 and was linked to Place Garibaldi by the Rue Cassini. The Port of Nice was concerned mainly with the transit of goods: Italian oils and agricultural crops (vegetables, lemons, oranges, anchovies and sardines from the county of Nice, rice, hemp silk from the Piedmont) and tanned skins for export. In addition, to meet the requirements of a rapidly growing town, corn from Russia, Algeria and North America was imported, along with exotic produce like sugar, cocoa, spices and coffee.

HOW TO GET THERE

Bus: N°. 3,7,9,10,14,20,27,30,81,82 - Bus stop : Le Port

WHAT TO SEE

We recommend a stroll around the Port area to see the houses belonging to the great merchant families of Nice in the 18th and 19th centuries on the Rue Ségurane, Rue Cassini and on the quays (see map page 6) as well as the church Notre-Dame-du-Port. Itinerary: The walk begins at The Ponchettes, passing by the Quai Rauba Capèu, the Quai Lunel and the Quai des Docks. Take the main central staircase behind the fountain to access the Place Ile-de-Beauté. After visiting the church, turn to your left into Rue Cassini to arrive at Place Garibaldi (see page 42). NB. Not far from the Port is the Museum of Prehistory Terra Amata (page 62) and the Lazaret Caves (page 65).

9

PLACE GARIBALDI

FROM THE MIDDLE AGES TO NAPOLEON III

Piazza Vittoria (Place Garibaldi) was built for Victor-Amédée III, King of Piedmont-Sardinia, as a royal entry into Nice for the Route Royale from Turin and to link the Old Town to the port and the new districts across the river. Remains of the city's medieval fortifications were found under the square in 2006 during work on the tramway. They can be visited in the custom-designed archaeological crypt-museum. Place Garibaldi, with its baroque painted facades and Italianate arcades, has recently been restored to its original glory.

WHAT TO SEE
The square, the Chapel of St-Sépulcre, the crypt

DISTRICT
Garibaldi – see map page 8

DATES
14th - 18th centuries

The Porte Pairolière: a Bulwark against Invasion

When the team of archaeologists, led by Marc Bouiron, Director of the Archaeology Service of Nice, commenced excavations in 2006 during the construction of the tram line, little did they expect to make a find of such magnitude. The site of the remains of the Porte Pairolière, one of the medieval city's three main gates, below the Place Garibaldi, is unbelievably well preserved. It encompasses the 14th century tower with its entire defence system: a moat, a 15th century ravelin (triangular fortification) and a 16th century bastion and its later reinforcements, which may be seen in a specially designed crypt-museum between the Boulevard Jean-Jaurès and the Place Garibaldi. The

Place Garibaldi - **Photo by Pierre Behar**

INTERVIEW

THE ARCHAEOLOGICAL CRYPT AND ITS ANCIENT REMAINS

Marc Bouiron

(Archéologist)

Marc Bouiron is Curator of Cultural Heritage and Director of the Archaeology Service of the City of Nice. He directed the archaeological dig on the Place Garibaldi during the construction of the tramway.

Can you describe the archaeological crypt?

The crypt which has been created beneath the tracks of the tram line is an impressive piece of construction work. Built in ferro-cement, 80 meters long and 10 meters wide, it was designed to display the remains of the medieval city's entire defence system which ranges from the rampart dating from the end of the 13th century to the 17th moat which protected the Saint-Sébastien bastion of the *Porte Pairolière* and includes examples of the evolution of military architecture over this several hundred year period. It is an extremely important heritage site for the City of Nice and has been listed as an historic monument.

How old are the most ancient remains found during the dig?

During the dig, we opened up a "window" below the medieval archaeological levels which revealed a wall running parallel to the River Paillon, together with other related levels. The ceramics found in this stratigraphic sequence date back to the end of Antiquity, probably to the 5th century A.D. The wall is the remains of a construction that was close to, but not in direct contact with, the river, probably a terrace wall which is linked to the ancient city of *Nikaïa*. To date, archaeological relics of this outpost of the Greek city of Marseille are extremely rare finds and do not enable us to locate the town (which is a completely separate entity from *Cemenelum* - see page 66) with any precision. This find is therefore particularly significant, even if it is more than likely that we are on the outskirts of the ancient city.

The lower part of the tower (Tour Pairolière) which probably dates from the 1380's. Photo by Marc Bouiron

Place Garibaldi - Decorative Trompe l'Oeil Facades

two other town gates, the Porte Saint-Eloi and the Porte du Pont, gave access respectively to the old port of Saint-Lambert in the south-east, and to the right bank of the river via the Old Bridge (Pont-Vieux) to the west. The Porte de la Pairolière was the sole access to the north and the main thoroughfares towards Lympia (marshes and farmland at the time), Villefranche (then the main port of Nice), the Paillon valley and the road to Turin. As a strategic point of passage, the role of the Porte de la Pairolière was clear: to defend the city from potential assaillants and a number of battles were fought on this historic site, for example, in 1543, during the Franco-Turkish siege of Nice. Legend tells of a young laundress, Catherine Ségurane, who, on 15th August 1543, brandishing a flag she had just seized from a soldier, beat back the enemy with her laundry bat. She naturally became one of Nice's heroines and, in 1923, a monument was erected in her honour Rue Sincaire.

Place Garibaldi since 1782

Plans were made in 1773 by Victor-Amédée III, King of Piedmont-Sardinia, to modernise the road (*Route Royale*) from the capital, Turin, with a fittingly regal entry into Nice. The construction of a great square commenced in 1782. Initially, named after the Porte Pairolière close by, it was renamed Place Victor (*Piazza Vittoria*) in honour of the king who had inspired these ambitious projects. On 13th September 1860, the Emperor Napoléon III and his wife,

Eugénie, arrived on Place Victor, now renamed Place Napoléon, for an official celebration of the reunification of the County of Nice (*Comté de Nice*) with France. They were greeted by huge crowds who had come from all over the county to attend the ceremony during which the Emperor was presented with the key to the city. A temporary monumental triumphal arch had been erected for the occasion. Ten years later, in 1870, the square was given its present name in honour of Giuseppe Garibaldi, born in Nice and hero of the struggle for Italian unification (creation of the Italian state). Place Garibaldi has always been at the heart of important commercial activity with its shops and restaurants and the transit of goods between the port and the Old Town. The square, with its ochre facades and their magnificent trompe-l'oeil frescoes in the baroque style, has been meticulously restored (2008 - 2012) making it unique today in Europe.

The Chapel of Saint-Sépulcre (in the background) and the statue of Garibaldi (to the fore).

A Marriage of Styles: Baroque and Neo-Classical

The Place Garibaldi was designed in the late eighteenth century by Antonio Spinelli. Marrying baroque and neo-Classical architecture, the vast rectangular square was bordered on all four sides by imposing buildings with arcades in the manner of the great squares of Turin. The yellow-ochre rather plain facades were painted with trompe l'oeil frescoes to create an illusion of grandeur and wealth. The magnificent neo-classical facade of the Chapel du Saint-Sépulcre, home to the Brotherhood of Blue Penitents, was designed to catch the eye of the visitor arriving on the square from Turin (Avenue de la République). The chapel's resplendent interior is a remarkable example of baroque art in the *Comté de Nice* (see page 74), achieving an impression of volume and space despite its cramped location on the narrow first floor of the building.

HOW TO GET THERE

Place Garibaldi
Tramway N°. 1
Tramstop: Garibaldi
Bus: N°. 3, 7, 9, 10, 14, 27, T32, 81, 82
Bus stop : Ségurane

Chapel of the Holy Sepulchre
Address: Place Garibaldi. Open every Sunday for mass at 6.30 p.m. The chapel may also be visited by appointement: Tel : 06 12 75 94 02.

The Archaeological Crypt
Address: Place Jacques Toja. Open Wednesday to Sunday on reservation at the Centre du Patrimoine, 75 Quay des États-Unis. Entry: 5€
Tel : 04 92 00 41 90.

WHAT TO SEE

The statue in honour of Garibaldi in the centre of the square, the Chapel du Saint-Sépulcre and the Archaeological Crypte (medieval and modern fortifications).

10

MAMAC

MUSEUM OF MODERN ART AND CONTEMPORARY ART

The Museum of Modern Art and Contemporary Art (MAMAC) was opened in Nice in 1990. Its imposing silhouette of elegant white and grey marble greets visitors from the top of Nice's new inner-city park, the *Promenade du Paillon*. The Museum is part of a single architectural unit which includes the National Theatre of Nice, the Louis Nucera public library and the *Promenade des Arts* raised walkway. The museum's collections cover works from the New European Realists and the School of Nice to the American movements of Pop Art and Abstract Expressionism.

WHAT TO SEE
The museum collections

DISTRICT
Garibaldi – see map page 6

DATES
20th and 21st Centuries

The Museum as a Work of Art

In 1987, an agreement was signed between the City of Nice and the French State for funding of a new Art museum together with the acquisition of artworks over a five-year period. The project, entrusted to the architects, Bayard and Vidal, included the museum (MAMAC), a theatre (*Théâtre National de Nice*) and a public Library (*Bibliothèque Louis Nucéra*) linked by a raised esplanade. The city-centre location of the site left the architects no choice but to build upwards. The building that emerged, in the form of a a tetrapod arch spanning the River Paillon (under cover), consists of four monolithic square towers, 20 meters wide by 30 meters high, linked by glass-walled corridors. The design, with its red-ochre base and rows of olive trees outlined against the towers' blank facades of white polished Carrara marble, takes its inspiration

MAMAC with the *Tête Carrée* by Sacha Sosno to the fore

INTERVIEW

MAMAC AND THE SCHOOL OF NICE

Gilbert Perlein

(Curator)

Mr Perlein is the Curator of the Museum of Modern Art and Contemporary Art of Nice.

What are the aims of the museum and what, in particular, has contributed to its success with the public?

The mission of the MAMAC is to collect, preserve and make available to the general public, artworks and objects from the 1950's to the present day through permanent and temporary exhibitions. The Museum's collection represents the multiplicity of art forms over the past sixty years with a special interest in the art of assemblage and assembled objects. The MAMAC's documentation centre collects and preserves documents specializing in contemporary art. The region's wealth of creativity has changed the course of the museum's programme which now has a double mission that is simultaneously regional and international. We have around 180,000 visitors a year which is sizeable for a museum outside Paris!

Where does the School of Nice stand in modern Art?

The term "School of Nice" (*École de Nice*) was coined *a posteriori* to designate the group of artists and creators on the scene in Nice in the 1960's to 1970's, sometimes even the 1980's. When the term emerged, Klein was already no longer with us, Arman was living in the States, Martial Raysse and others didn't want to hear about it. And yet, they were the creative force behind an unprecedented artistic emulation which completely turned art history on its head. If these artists had been able to make a breakthrough, it is because they were open to the outside world. The main purpose of the the MAMAC is to set up a dialogue between the region and a much vaster story that is international in scope.

The MAMAC (below right) at the gates of the Old Town - **Photo: Pierre Behar**

from several sources : vernacular Mediterranean, Belle-Époque and Classical architecture (square plan and arch) which echo the style of the adjacent Place Garibaldi. The exhibition space extends over three levels with additional space on the roof terraces from where the public can admire the panoramic views over the city and the Old Town. Yves Klein's "Mur du Feu", commissioned by the *Musées de France*, occupies one of the terraces. This spectacular work, which comes to life on special events nights at the museum, lines up rows of Bunsen burners which, when lit, burst into blue flower-shaped flames. The main entrance, the museum shop, the auditorium and the museum gallery are accessed from the esplanade, which is itself an open air museum for a number of sculptures by Alexander Calder (*Stabile Mobile*), Niki de Saint Phalle (*The Loch Ness Monster*) and Jonathan Borofsky (*The Man with the Suitcase*).

Art in All its Forms

The City of Nice commissioned monumental works by four international artists for the interior courtyard which has exhibition space on four of the three-storey high walls. These installations highlight major works from the museum's collection with *Wall Drawing* XX 1004 *Arcs* (2002) by Sol LeWitt, a specialist in large scale frescoes (American movement of Abstract Expressionism), *Répétition* (2002) by Claude Viallat in which a stencilled shape is repeated over a coloured base (1970's Tachism movement within the French Abstract Expressionist School), *Camin dei Inglese* (2004) by Arman, a gigantic stack of recycled blue chairs from the Promenade des Anglais and, for the fourth wall, a 14.4 meters high detail from *Déjeuner sur l'herbe*, (1964) by Alain Jacquet, which has been enlarged to the extent that the original painting has become almost abstract.

The museum's permanent collection covers works from the 1950's to the present day. The School of Nice features in prominent position: Yves Klein who invented a fascinatingly intense blue, Ben who is famous for his message-paintings, César for his compressions and Arman for his assemblages of objects.... In 2001, Niki de Saint Phalle made a major donation of her works to the City of Nice. On the third floor of the museum, movements such as *Pop Art* with Andy Warhol or Lichtenstein, the *Minimal*, the *Color Field* and *Figuration Libre* are well represented. Temporary exhibitions are also organised within the museum space (and at other galleries in Nice, such as the *Galérie des Ponchettes*), as well as conferences and projections of art videos. An important function of the museum is to expose potential young artists to modern and contemporary art by organising visits to the museum by schools from the region.

HOW TO GET THERE

Address: Place Yves Klein. Open from 10 a.m. to 6 p.m. Closed on Monday and 1st January, Easter Sunday, 1st May, 25th December. Tel : 04 93 13 42 01.

Bus: N°. 4,7,9,10 - Bus stop : Defly - Klein
Bus: N°. 6,17,82 - Bus stop : Pont-Barla
Bus: N°. 16 - Bus stop : Promenade des Arts

WHAT TO SEE

In addition to the permanent and temporary shows at the MAMAC, visitors will discover a wealth of historical and cultural attractions close to the museum : the gardens of the *Promenade du Paillon* (see page 24), *La Tête Carrée* of the Louis Nucéra Municipal Library (see page 86), the 18th century Place Garibaldi (see page 42) and the Archeological Crypte for a glimpse of medieval Nice (see page 45).

11

CHAGALL
THE MUSEUM

A UNIVERSAL MESSAGE

The Musée National Marc Chagall was inaugurated by André Malraux on 7th July 1973, the artist's 86th birthday. The museum is home to the prodigious Biblical Message donated to the French State by Chagall and his wife. An artist rarely has a permanent museum dedicated to him during his lifetime, but Chagall had lived on the Côte d'Azur since the 1950's and this is where he wished to leave this major work, the bearer of a strong and universal message. "If all life leads inexorably to an end, we must colour our lives with love and hope. It is in love that the social logic of life and the essence of every religion reside."

DISTRICT
Cimiez – see map p. 7

DATES
20th Century

For Marc Chagall, The Bible is "The Greatest Source of Poetry of all Time"

Throughout his lifetime, Chagall mastered a wide range of techniques and materials : painting, murals, etching, lithography, ballet costumes and sets, ceramics, sculpture, stained-glass, tapestry and mosaics. He was a prolific, indefatigable artist whose work ranges from book engravings to monumental works such as the seventeen paintings of the Biblical Message inspired by Genesis, Exodus and The Song of Songs. "Perhaps the young and not so young will come to this House in search of an ideal of Fraternity and Love, such as I have dreamt with my colours and my lines." Chagall's exalted colours are perceived instantaneously, in the same way as music, leaving the spectator with a spontaneous reading of the artist's profoundly human vision.

Musée National Marc Chagall - Credit: Musées Nationaux du XXe siècle des Alpes-Maritimes, photo by P. Gérin

From Vitebsk to the Côte d'Azur, via Paris, Berlin and New-York

Marc Chagall would have a destiny that was as exceptional as it was unexpected. The eldest of nine children, he was born into a modest Jewish family in 1887 at Vitebsk, Belarus. His bold choice of colours and liberty of expression, unrestricted by "reality," were to set him apart at his first art classes, aged nineteen. He studied under Léon Bakst in Saint Petersburg, who advised him to go Paris, the centre of avant-garde art. He arrived in the French capital in 1911 and patronised the well known schools before moving into his own studio where he found himself surrounded by an "artistic bohemia" of every nationality. He worked at night, so that he could spend the days "discovering his craft", initially, at the Louvre with the classical great masters and later, at the Impressionist, Fauvist and Cubist exhibitions. Through their contact, he experimented with different techniques and a new palette of colours. Bakst who was visiting Paris, told him "Now your colours sing." During this formative period, rich in creativity and encounters, Chagall asserted his independence from any art movement, creating his own distinctive signature. His allegorical works composed in a brilliant rainbow of colours, bear the stamp of the Russian and Jewish cultures.

During the summer of 1914, Chagall went to Berlin for his first solo exhibition which met with great success. Without losing any time, he left for Vitebsk where Bella, his fiancée and muse, had been waiting for four years. The couple, caught up in the war that broke out and the Russian Revolution in 1917, would not leave again before 1922. During that period, however, Chagall would be hailed as one the major artists of his generation after several exhibitions in Petrograd and Moscow.

When Chagall finally returned to France, he found his studio devastated : nothing was left of the three years of work which had earnt him some international renown. Only a few of the 200 works shown at Berlin would be returned to him. He spent the next four years building up his main body of work again, painting replicas or variants of the originals. When the Chagalls were invited by the Museum of Modern Art to the safety of New York during the Second World War, the entire contents of his studio went with them (1,600 kg!). Back in France in 1948, he settled in the South captivated by the extraordinary light of the Côte d'Azur. He lived for many years at Vence and then Saint-Paul-de-Vence where he died aged 98.

The Museum

The minimalist style building designed by architect, André Hermant, set in a Mediterranean garden, offers visitors the perfect setting for the contemplation of Chagall's masterpieces. The artist created a tapestry for the entrance hall, a mosaic for the pool and stained-glass windows for the concert hall. Pieces representing the broad scope of Chagall's career, as well as a film library documenting his life are held by the Museum.

HOW TO GET THERE

Address: Avenue Docteur Ménard. Open from 10 a.m. to 6 p.m (May to October) and 10 a.m. to 5 p.m (November to April). Closed on Tuesday.

Tel : 04 93 53 87 20. There is an admission charge with a special tarif for temporary exhibitions. Free for under 26 year-olds and on the first Sunday of every month.

Bus: N°. 15,22 - Bus stop : Musée Chagall

12

RÉGINA
THE HOTEL EXCELSIOR

A PALACE* FIT FOR A QUEEN

The imposing Hôtel Excelsior Régina greets visitors in a fittingly regal manner from the top of the boulevard de Cimiez. Designed by the celebrated Niçois architect, Sébastien-Marcel Biasini; the lavish Belle-Époque hotel was patronised by Queen Victoria and her court. She stayed in a private wing at the Régina on three occasions for six weeks (1897-99). Converted into private apartments in 1934, the Régina was home to two other famous occupants: the artist Henri Matisse and the Niçois sculptor, Sacha Sosno.

WHAT TO SEE
The Belle-Époque facades and entrance

DISTRICT
Cimiez – see map p. 7

DATES
From 1897 to the present day

From Queen Victoria ...

Queen Victoria of Great Britain, stayed for six weeks at the Grand Hôtel, Cimiez in the spring of 1895. Her enthusiastic enjoyment of Nice caught the attention of the Niçois banker, Henri Germain, and a group of investors. Shortly after her departure, a vast building programme was launched: to build an exceptional hotel at Cimiez. The design was entrusted to the eminent architect, Sébastien-Marcel Biasini, with the mission to have the Royal wing ready for Victoria's next visit the following spring. Work on the foundations began in June, but the task was titanic and the hotel was finally inaugurated in Feburary 1897, only weeks before the arrival of the royal guest. A luxurious six-floor wing, accessed by an electrically operated lift, and adjoining gardens complete with exotic plants, tennis courts,

The Régina in the late 1890's. Crédit : Library of Congress Digital Gallery,. reproduction number LC-DIG-ppmsc-05002 (www.victorianweb.c

cycle path and croquet lawn were reserved for her exclusive use. A golden crown graces the domed roof in her honour. Throughout her three stays at the Régina, the daily court bulletin and laudatory articles published in the British newspapers were a fabulous source of publicity for the French Riviera. The Queen loved sallying forth in her carriage to visit the coast and the surrounding hills for the views and their wild beauty, or the Old Town to see the Carnival, a religious pageant or a military parade. As she left Nice in 1899, Victoria wrote in her journal "The morning was again beautiful and added to one's sadness at leaving. Every year, I grow fonder of dear Cimiez" (see page 110). It was to be her last visit.

... to Henri Matisse

The Régina, like other grand hotels located in town far from the sea-front, had built its successs on the winter tourist trade, which all but disappeared when summer seaside holidays became fashionable. The hotel closed and was transformed into apartments in 1934. Matisse had an apartment and his studio at the Régina from 1938 – 1954 (see page 54: Matisse in Nice). His young neighbour, Sacha Sosno, would, in turn, contribute to Nice's eminence as a city of Art (see page 86).

Biasini, Prominent Niçois Architect of the Belle-Époque

The brilliant architect and town planner, Sébastien-Marcel Biasini (1841 - 1913), was highly influential in Nice during the entire *Belle Époque* era. He designed many prestigious buildings, as varied in style as the Hôtel Excelsior Régina, the Palais de Marbre, the Crédit Lyonnais (Avenue Jean-Médecin) and the estate at Cimiez. Nicknamed "His Majesty Biasini", he was a flamboyant, fun-loving, energetic character who was well known in local life, as much for his poems in the Niçois dialect as for his designs of floats and grotesque figures for the Carnival of Nice.

The Belle Époque entrance to the Régina

* Since the 1890's, the term *Palace Hotel*, designates a grand luxury hotel. Palace is now an official rating in France for an exclusive selection of top class hotels.

HOW TO GET THERE

Address : 71-73 boulevard de Cimiez
Bus : N°. 15, 22, 24 – Bus stop : Victoria

WHAT TO SEE

The Régina is a private residence and may only be viewed from the exterior. However, the area offers a wealth of attractions : the Matisse Museum (see page 54), the Museum of Archaeology Nice-*Cemenelum* and the Roman baths and amphitheatre (see page 66), the Franciscan church and gardens, the cemetery of Cimiez (see page 106), the Belle Époque buildings and villas on the Boulevard de Cimiez (see page 81).

13

MATISSE THE MUSEUM

NICE: AN ARTIST'S INSPIRATION

The Matisse Museum stands in a park of olive trees bordering the Roman ruins of *Cemenelum*. The 17th century Genoese style villa which has housed the museum since 1963,was modernised and extended in 1993. The museum's permanent collection covers the entire range of Matisse's output, giving the viewer special insight into his artistic research, breakthroughs and progressions in the fields of colour and graphics from his very first paintings (1890) to the gouache paper decoupages (1953), a technique he developed at the end of his life.

WHAT TO SEE
The Villa and Museum

DISTRICT
Cimiez – see map p.7

DATES
17th and 20th centuries

The Museum and a Genoese Villa

In 1950, the City of Nice acquired the The *Villa des Arènes*, an aristocratic 17th century Genoese villa with red-ochre facades painted in trompe-l'oeil. In 1963, it became home to the Museum of Archaeology and, on the first floor, to collections donated by Matisse and his heirs. When the archaeology section moved out onto the adjacent site of the ancient Roman city, the villa was converted by the architect, Jean-François Bodin to accommodate the new Matisse Museum. His streamlined design, in keeping with his philosophy of "rigour, elegance and singularity", retained the villa's stunning original facades, opened up new exhibition spaces and added a new wing on two levels. The lower level, accessed by a wide open-air staircase, is laid out

The Genoese Villa, now the Matisse Museum

M.T. Pulvénis de Séligny

(Curator)

Madame Pulvénis de Séligny is Curator of the Matisse Museum, Cimiez.

Can you describe Matisse's production during his years on the Côte d'Azur?

Matisse's production during his years on the Côte d'Azur is of capital importance and is particularly diverse. One example is the series, *Les Odalisques*, painted in his apartment on the Cours Saleya against an sumptuous backcloth of screens, moucharaby latticework and drapes. The Chapelle du Rosaire, which the artist himself considered to be his masterpiece, is the culmination of his lifetime quest to achieve harmony and balance. The monumental compositions of gouache cut-outs were created when he lived at the Régina. He drew directly onto the the ceiling and the walls of his bedroom using a bamboo pole. His last works, produced between 1950 – 1953: *Danseuse créole*, *La Vague*, *Nu bleu* IV *and Fleurs et fruits*, are part of the Museum's collection today.

Was there a reciprocal relationship between Nice and the region and the artist?

Matisse worked almost permanently in Nice from 1920, continually renewing his reflection and exploring his craft. "Most people are drawn here for the light and because it is picturesque. Coming from the North, what made up my mind was the way that, in January, the colours are reflected so intensely and the brilliance of the light." (interview by Yves Bridault for *Arts magazine*, 1952. President of Honour of the *Union Méditerranéenne pour l'Art Moderne*), Matisse played in influential rôle for artists and modern art in Nice. In particular, he personally oversaw the creation of the Ponchettes Gallery.

What were the reactions to Matisse's first exhibitions in Nice?

When Matisse's first exhibition was held at the Palais de la Méditerranée in 1946, the reception was lukewarm. It was not until his second exhibition in 1950 at the new Ponchettes Gallery of 38 paintings, drawings, sculptures and tapestries, that the public really discovered the genius of his work.

General view of a room of the permanent exhibition with *Nu bleu IV*, 1952, *La Serpentine*, 1909, and *Vitrail*, a study for *L'Arbre de Vie* for the Chapelle de la Rosaire, Vence, 1950 - Credit : H. Matisse Legacy for the artist's works. Photo :Ville de Nice, Musée Matisse.

The Matisse Museum

around Matisse's monumental gouache paper cut-out, *Flowers and Fruit* (1953), one of his last works. The museum was inaugurated in 1993.

A Great Artist is Born – the Paris Years

Henri Émile Benoît Matisse was born on 31 December 1869 at Cateau-Cambrésis, Nord-Pas-de-Calais. The son of a grain merchant, he studied law and was employed as a solicitor's clerk. It was during a long period of convalescence that, aged twenty, thanks to a box of paints his mother had given him to occupy the long days, he discovered the joys of painting. He moved to Paris to study art with Gustave Moreau at the *École des Beaux-Arts*, where he received an education in classical art, copying the Old Masters at the Louvre and learning to sculpt. Matisse rapidly gained a reputation as a defiant student as his style changed through contact with the contemporary art movements and artists such as Russell, Cézanne, Gauguin and Van Gogh. His experiments lead to the creation of a new group who were dubbed *Les Fauves* (meaning "wild beasts") by a shocked critic in reaction to the bold, "unnatural" colours of works exhibited by Matisse, Derain, Manguin, Marquet and Vlaminck at the Paris 1905 *Salon d'Automne*. It was for Matisse, nonetheless, the beginning of a period of some acclaim with work shown at Berlin, Moscow, London, Munich and New York, and, with a new material comfort, the chance to travel.

Nice, an Endless Source of Inspiration

Matisse arrived at the Hôtel Beau Rivage overlooking the Bay of Nice in December 1918. His doctor had prescribed the warm sun of the Côte d'Azur to cure his bronchitis, but Matisse was out of luck. It rained for the entire month (one of his still lifes depicted an umbrella in a bucket). In exasperation, Matisse packed his bags; but the next morning he was greeted by brilliant sunshine, revealing the Côte d'Azur's extraordinary quality of light and dazzling array of colours. "When I realised that I would wake up every morning to that light, I couldn't believe my good fortune." (Preface of the exhibition Henri Matisse, Nice, 1950 – Georges Salles). Matisse rented an apartment close to the hotel where he set up his studio. Several months later, he stayed in a villa on the Mont Boron from where he could marvel at the sunrise illuminating the bay and the roofs of Old Nice below. From 1921, he took up residence in the Palais de Caïs de Pierlas overlooking the market stalls at the far end of the Cours Saleya, before acquiring two apartments, in 1938, at the Régina (the hotel built at Cimiez for Queen Victoria – see page 52), where he lived and worked. That year, he designed costumes and scenery for the Montecarlo Ballets Russes.

In 1941, Matisse had an operation for cancer and was expected to live for only six months. He could not walk and had to remain seated, often working in bed. Undeterred, his work output continued to be prolific and two years later, he moved to Villa *Le Rêve* in Vence to escape the War and the bombs, only returning five years later, in January 1949, to the Régina to compose the murals for his major project, the *Chapelle du Rosaire* at Vence (1951). He died at the Régina on 3 November 1954 and was buried at the cemetary at Cimiez (see page 106).

Window with shutters at the Matisse Museum

HOW TO GET THERE

Address: Musée Matisse, 164, avenue des Arènes de Cimiez. Open from 10 a.m. to 6 p.m. Closed on Tuesday and certain public holidays. Entrance free.
Tel : 04 93 81 08 08.
Bus: N°. 15, 17, 22, 24 - Bus stop : Musée Matisse

WHAT TO SEE

The permanent exhibition takes the visitor through the development of Matisse's style from his earliest works (*Nature morte aux livres*, 1890, signed Essitam) to his gouache paper cut-outs (*Danseuse créole*, *Nu bleu* IV, *Fleurs et fruits*), including drawings, engravings, sculptures and finally, his sketches and maquettes for the *Chapelle du Rosaire* at Vence.

14

ARSON THE VILLA

ART SCHOOL AND CENTRE FOR CONTEMPORARY ART

Villa Arson Visual Arts School is a public institution dedicated to contemporary art. It opened in 1972 under the auspices of the Ministry of Culture with multiple missions to teach, carry out research, facilitate innovatory projects and international exchange, and bring the newest artistic techniques to the public via exhibitions and events. The modern architectural complex encompasses the Arson family country villa and gardens in the Saint-Barthélémy district of Nice. It was awarded the "20th Century Heritage Label" in 2003.

WHAT TO SEE
The Villa, gardens, artworks, and exhibitions

DISTRICT
Saint-Barthélémy (Nice-Nord)

DATES
18th - 21th centuries

Pierre-Joseph Arson

The villa takes its name from Pierre-Joseph Arson, a prosperous merchant and royalist from Avignon, who had fled from the French Revolution to settle in the port district of Nice. In 1812, he bought the sumptuous 18th century Italianate villa on the hill at Saint-Barthélémy (now Nice Nord) from the Consul of Nice, Peyre de la Coste. The Arson family set about embellishing their new country residence and, in particular, creating a vast Italian style pleasure garden with elegant terraces, statues, balustrades and baroque fountains and planted with exotic palms, aloes, citrus and cacti in amongst the indigenous pines, carob and olive trees. In 1824, the great French diplomat Talleyrand admiring the remarkable views from the Villa Arson is said to have exclaimed "Had I known this was such a beautiful country, it

The Villa Arson

INTERVIEW

PREPARING CREATIVE INNOVATION FOR TOMORROW

Yves Robert
(Director)

Mr Yves Robert is the former Director of the Villa Arson.

What are the artistic goals of the Villa Arson?
Villa Arson was part of Minister André Malraux's grand plan to reform the teaching of art in France. This public institution of higher education combines a national visual arts school and campus, a centre for contemporary art, a multimedia library and a residence for guest artists. The special role of the Villa Arson School of Visual Arts is to not only teach art but to also provide support for research projects into contemporary creative activity and contribute to cultural diffusion. The exceptional facilities offered by Villa Arson allow future artists to train in the sphere of the visual arts using the newest artistic practices, benefitting from continual contact with studio-led research projects and the working artists and professionals living on site. The students who are recruited by an entrance examination, follow a five year curriculum which leads to two state diplomas. The opportunities for dialogue with professional artists and the technical and theoretical training provided, enables each student to construct their own project as a future artist.

How does Villa Arson work and what are the projects in the offing?
Villa Arson's teaching is interdisciplinary and functions within a synergy between the school, the art centre and the artists-in-residence. The art centre, which is open to the public, puts on a programme of exhibitions organised around a research project designed to produce works of international exhibition quality. These can be both collaborative innovative exhibitions and monographic exhibitions featuring young emerging artists. It is the school's mission to explore and invent what could be tomorrow's creation. The school also has the aim to reach out to the widest possible audience and into the region. Villa Arson is also an historic site with a strong heritage. Its gardens and terraces offer an exceptional viewpoint over the city. We want the public to feel at home at the Villa Arson to enjoy the views, to walk in the grounds and to experience new artistic encounters.

View of Nice from the gardens of the Villa Arson in 1860.
Watercolour by Urbain Garin de Cocconato - Bibliothèque du Chevalier de Cessole-Nice

wouldn't be in the hands of the King of Sardinia..." (Nice was part of the House of Savoy Piedmont and Sardinia from 1388 to 1860, except for several short periods E.g. 1793 - 1814 - during the French Revolution). Talleyrand had represented France at the Congress of Vienna when the return of Nice to the House of Savoy was negotiated in 1814). Pierre-Joseph died in 1851 leaving the property to his son.

The Intractable Louis-Gonzague Arson

The Chevalier Louis-Gonzague Arson, son of Pierre-Joseph, was a lawyer. In 1855, he embarked on a career in journalism, founding a newspaper entitled *La Terre Promise* (The Promised Land) or the *Gazette de Nice* with the Republican Alphonse Karr who had also taken refuge at Nice. Like his father before him, Louis-Gonzague was hostile to the reunification of Nice with France and even fought a duel with another journalist who was pro-France. His newspaper played an active role in the public debate in the run-up to the 1860 referendum when the people of Nice were asked if they wanted to join France. With his English wife, Jamina Taylor-Travers, Louis-Gonzague continued to embellish the Arson family country villa where they entertained distinguished guests such as Maximilien de Bavière and the Queen of Wurtemberg.

Michel Marot's Visionary Project

The villa was acquired by the City of Nice in 1964 and donated to the State for the construction of an international art school according to the wishes of André Malraux, then Minister for Culture. A year later, the

project of architect, Michel Marot, co-designer of the *Marina Baie des Anges* at Villeneuve-Loubet, was selected. The architectural programme included the art school together with an exhibition centre, a multimedia library, student and artists' residences, lecture halls, studios and a restaurant. Although several stories high and covering a staggering three quarters of the surface area of the park, particular attention was paid to merge the constructions into the natural hillside setting. To further soften the visual impact, the walls were either left as rough shuttered concrete or faced with pebbles from the Var River and the roofs were transformed into Mediterranean gardens recalling the former park's numerous terraces. The buildings, in the form of interconnected cubes, are organised around three striking features: the 18th century villa which, with its warm red-ochre façade, is highlighted as the centrepiece of the complex, a monumental central staircase, and a series of patios which introduce sunlight and air into the interior and offset the trees preserved from the original garden (not a single tree was felled).
The Villa Arson, incorporating the *École Nationale des Arts décoratifs de Nice* founded in 1881 and the *Centre artistique de rencontres internationales*, was inaugurated on 20th May 1972. In 1986, the school was renamed *Ecole pilote internationale d'art et de la recherche* associated with the *Centre national d'art contemporain* founded and directed by Henri Maccheroni (aided by Michel Butor). In 2006, the Ministry for Culture and Communications began a restoration programme to reopen the terraces and gardens to the public.

The Gardens

At the beginning of the 20th century, part of the garden was lost when the villa was transformed into a hotel. Only the maritime pines and avenue of cyprus trees remain from the Arson family era. The plants and trees, the majority of which are Mediterranean species, are an important part of the new architectural design and the sense of balance between the constructions and the garden gives this site its exceptional character.

HOW TO GET THERE

Address : 20 avenue Stephen Liégeard. Tel : 04 92 07 73 73.
The Villa Arson, its Art Centre, gardens and terraces are open to the public every day, except Monday and Tuesday, from 14h to 18h (14h to 19h in July and August). Closed on the 1st May, 25th December and the 1st January.

Bus : N°. 7, 4 – Bus stop : Deux Avenues
Cross the Avenue Cyrille Besset at the crossroads with the Boulevard de Cessole and turn into the Avenue Stephen Liégeard.
Tram N°. 1 : tram stop : Le Ray, then a ten minute signed walk along the Rue Paul Mellarède and Rue Joseph d'Arbaud.

WHAT TO SEE

The 18th century villa, its Mediterranean gardens and magnificent olive trees are really worth a visit. Michel Marot's design centred on the theme of opening out to the exterior and the free circulation of air and light mirrors the school ethos. There is continual dialogue and exchange between the students and their learning environment.

NICE AND PREHISTORY

400,000 YEARS OF HISTORY!

Southeastern France has a rich history of prehistoric occupation of at least one million years (Vallonnet Cave). Traces found at Nice of early Man, dating back 400,000 years, may be seen at the permanent exhibition of the world renowned Terra Amata site-museum close to the Port. Not far from Terra Amata are the Lazaret Caves where Homo Erectus settled 170,000 years ago and in the Cimiez and Caucade districts, two other sites have provided evidence of the arrival of the first farmers and herders in the Neolithic.

WHAT TO SEE
The Museum of Terra Amata and the Lazaret Cave

DATES
From the Lower Palaeolithic to Neolithic

The site of Terra Amata is known the world over. Why?

Nice has one of the most famous prehistoric sites in the world. Scientists come from as far as Corea, Georgia and Chili to visit Terra Amata which, together with two or three other European sites, has produced evidence of the oldest hearths in the history of Humanity. The domestication of fire, 400,000 years ago, is one of the most important phases in Man's evolution. It brought about a fundamental change to the lifestyle of *Homo Erectus* and ultimately to the species itself. As well as providing light and heat, fire improved food (plants and meat were easily digested) and prevented illness. It meant that the clan spent time eating together around the campfire which promoted social exchange and the transmission of knowledge. Fire became

General view of the archaeological site of Terra Amata during excavations in 1966. Photo: Henry de Lumley/Museum of Terra Amata

A WALK INTO PREHISTORY

Two of the four prehistoric sites described below may be seen and both are of major scientific interest. Visits to the Terra Amata Museum of Human Palaeontology and the Lazaret Cave will take you on a journey through 300,000 years of history to discover the first humans (*Homo Erectus*) to have arrived in Nice and where and how they lived. The two sites are within a ten minute walk of each other and guarantee a fascinating day out. N.B. The Lazaret Cave can only be visited in July and August (the best time to see it, since the annual campaign of excavations are in full swing) (see page 65). Although the Giribaldi and Caucade sites cannot be visited, exhibitions presenting the sites may be seen at the Museum of Archaeology Nice-*Cemenelum* for Giribaldi (see page 66) and the Regional Museum of Prehistory at Menton for Caucade.

380,000 year old hearth discovered on one Terra Amata's archaeological levels. Photo: Terra Amata Museum of Human Palaeontology/City of Nice

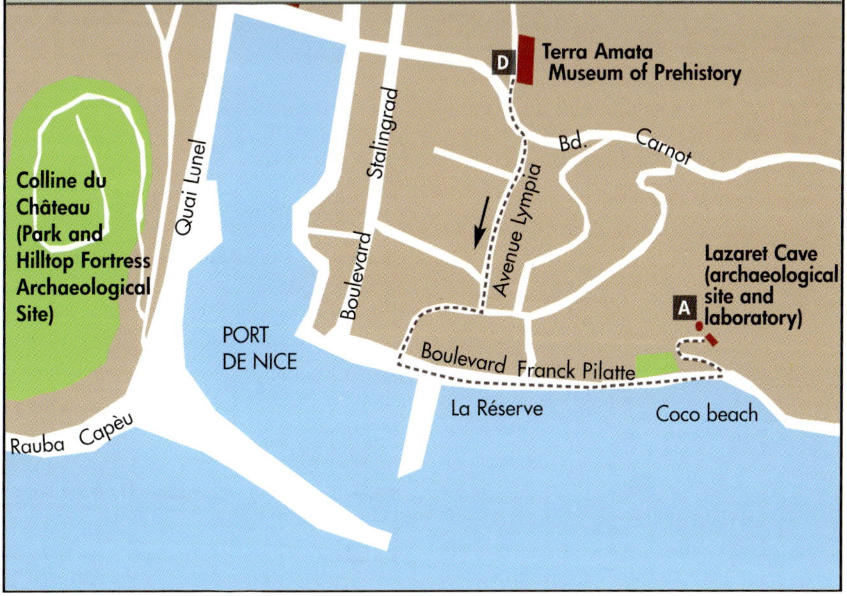

General view of the archaeological site of the Lazaret Cave where the transition between the Homo erectus and Neanderthal cultures is under investigation.
Photo: The Lazaret Departmental Laboratory of Prehistory

an important element of socialisation and, last but not least, fire put a distance between Man and Animal, literally and figuratively. With light after dark, he no longer depended on the cycle of day and night. This gave him control over his time and freed him from the circadian cycle.

Who were the men who came to the beach at Terra Amata?

400,000 years ago, Terra Amata was a pebble beach in a cove at the mouth of the River Paillon. A group of Prehistoric hunters camped here at the beginning of summer, returning over a number of years. They built a large hut with branches, made fires and manufactured stone tools (choppers, picks, hatchets, and hand axes) mostly from pebbles they found on the beach. These men hunted large herbivorous mammals typical of a temperate climate : young elephant, rhinoceros, aurochs, wildboar, deer and rabbit.

Terra Amata, a Model for French Site-Museums

The museum of Terra Amata was founded in 1976 on the archaeological site of the same name. It was the first site-museum in France and became a model for other museums attached to important archaeological research laboratories. The preventive archaeological dig, directed by Professor Henry de Lumley in 1966, lasted for six months and was a race against time prior to the construction of an apartment building. 150 young researchers, students and volunteers worked in relays day and night on the dig with the following results : 29 occupation levels were excavated, 28,800 objects were recorded on the site plan, washed and catalogued; in all, 70,000 objects were preserved and moulds made of 90m^2 of archaeological floors. Today, the collection is stored in 1,200 drawers in the museum archives. The results of more than four decades of research can be seen at the Terra Amata Museum of Human Palaeontology (see HOW TO GET THERE).

The Lazaret Prehistoric Hunters' Cave

Archaeologists from the Lazaret Departmental Laboratory of Prehistory have been excavating the cave for over fifty years under the scientific direction of Professor Henry de Lumley. The site serves as a reference for our knowledge of the evolution of the climate and the environment as well as of human culture and the life-style of nomad hunting communities who lived on the coast of the Alpes-Maritimes between 220,000 years and 130,000 years ago. During the 2011 summer campaign of excavations, a 170,000 year-old fragment of a young adult male hominin skull was found which will enable a major step forward in the puzzle regarding the evolution of Homo Erectus towards Neanderthal Man. A child's milk tooth found in November 2013, supports the hypothesis that the cave was not merely a hunters' encampment but was used to shelter whole families. The site has also revealed a great number of knapped stone tools (pebble implements, flakes and handaxes), as well as the remains of a rich and varied fauna, evidence of a cool and humid continental climate and a landscape with open grassy plains interspersed with extensive areas of forest. During the coldest periods of the Lazaret occupation, the men hunted deer, ibex, wild horse and bison, woolly rhinoceros, reindeer, marmots and wolverines which lived in the area surrounding the cave. Some of the archaeological levels indicate a more temperate climate when the hunted game were typical of forest species: cervidae, auroch and straight-tusked elephant.

HOW TO GET THERE

Terra Amata – The Museum
Address: 25, Boulevard Carnot. Open from 10 a.m. to 6 p.m. Closed on Monday and certain public holidays. Entrance free.
Tel : 04 93 55 59 57.
Bus: N°. 81 - Bus stop : Gustavin
Bus: N°. T32 - Bus stop : Carnot

Lazaret – The Cave
Address: 33bis, boulevard Franck Pilatte. The cave is not open to the public. However, it can be visited during the summer campagne of excavations in July and August and on European Heritage Days.

Tel : 04 92 00 17 37.

Bus: N°. 30, T32 - Bus stop : Villa La Cote

Giribaldi – The Site
The site cannot be visited. A presentation can be seen at the Museum of Archaeology Nice – *Cemenelum* and Gallo-Roman Site.
Address: 160, avenue des Arènes. Open from 10 a.m. to 6 p.m. Closed on Tuesday and certain public holidays. Entrance free. (see page 69).
Tel : 04 93 81 59 57.

Giribaldi and Caucade

The site at Caucade discovered during the construction of a road, has provided evidence of the arrival 5,000 years ago in the Alpes-Maritimes of the first farmers and herders. The Giribaldi site at Cimiez revealed remains of a dozen houses surrounded by cultivated fields, most probably a village, as well as clay pits for the manufacture of ceramics or for building adobe houses, dating back to 4500 B.C. The research conducted on material collected has resulted in a considerable amount of information regarding the evolution of the life-style of the first farming communities between 4700 and 4000 B.C. in Western Provence.

NICE DURING ANTIQUITY

BETWEEN *CEMENELUM* AND *NIKAÏA*

During the Roman Empire, the city of *Cemenelum* was founded next to an already established Greek sea-trading colony, *Nikaïa*. Both were within the perimeter of today's Nice. Towards the end of the 7th century, the Roman city was gradually abandoned in favour of the developing coastal town of Nice. Remains of *Cemenelum* are still standing in the Cimiez district: an amphitheatre, parts of a thermal spa, and in the museum of archaeology, some of the most significant finds from the site are on display. To date, no substantial evidence of *Nikaïa* can be visited.

WHAT TO SEE
The Museum, the baths, the amphitheatre

DISTRICT
Cimiez – see map page 7

DATES
1st century B.C. to 7th century A.D.

Cemenelum and *Nikaïa* : Rome, a stone's throw from Athens!

During Antiquity, barely three kilometres separated *Cemenelum* from *Nikaïa*. Prior to the arrival of the Romans, the former was inhabited by native Celto-Ligurians: the *Vediantians*, whereas the latter was a colony founded by Marseille. *Cemenelum*'s destiny would be taken in hand by the Romans, *Nikaïa*'s Greek identity would prevail for a long time. The city which the Roman emperor, Augustus, established towards the end of the 1st century, has yet to be fully investigated since only a small area including three bath houses, an amphitheatre, some streets and several shops, has been identified. The site of *Nikaïa*, which is thought to be in the vicinity of the hill (*Colline du Château*), is still an open question. Palaeo-Christian ceramics found

A Roman paved street which may be visited (south of the spa) at Cimiez

A WALK INTO ANTIQUITY

Visit the permanent exhibition of objects excavated from the site of *Cemenelum* at Nice's Museum of Archaeology at Cimiez. The amphitheatre located close to the entrance of the park is open to the public (see HOW TO GET THERE on page 69). Also, not to be missed, is the archaeological site on the hill (*Colline du Château*), which continues to be excavated every summer, and where the foundations of Nice's first early Christian cathedral dating back to the 5th century A.D. have been uncovered (see page 71).

A Roman oil lamp found at *Cemenelum*, depicting a woman bathing, is on show at the Museum of Archaeology.

(Photo: D. Taland, Museum of Nice - *Cemenelum*)

on the site have revealed that between Late Antiquity and the Early Middle Ages (5th and 7th centuries A.D.), *Cemenelum* and Nice were two independent bishoprics, the first of which was attached to Arles and the second to Marseille. After that, *Cemenelum* gradually disappeared off the map, leaving "medieval" Nice to grow in importance.

The West Baths at *Cemenelum*, built during the 2nd century A.D.

The Amphitheatre at *Cemenelum*, built during the 1st century A.D.

The North Baths at *Cemenelum*

Cemenelum : From Capital City of the Alpes-Maritimae to Ruins and Farmland

During the Roman period, the population of *Cemenelum* probably reached 30,000 inhabitants. The town was organised around the major public buildings (the forum, amphitheatre, baths, etc) and the places of worship (*necropoli*, temples, etc). Residential districts (*insulae*) were built into the space between these different monuments. The entire town was surrounded either by ramparts or moats. Remains of the *Via Julia Augusta* which traversed Menton and *Cemenelum* can be seen not far from the vicinity of the Grimaldi Caves on the Italian border. After the inhabitants of *Cemenelum* migrated to Nice at the end of the Roman period, the former capital city fell into ruins and the land reverted to fields and farms.

The Roman Baths at Cimiez

The archaeological site of Cimiez (*Cemenelum*) contains the ruins of three *thermae* (complexes of public baths): the North Baths, built in the 1st century A.D. are the the largest and most ancient baths of the complex. The East Baths were built a century later and, it is believed that the West (or New) Baths were built in the 3rd century A.D.. During Late Antiquity, these were converted into a church/cathedral with a baptistery in the northern part. Designed on the same model as the splendid baths in Rome, those of *Cemenelum* were decorated with precious marbles from Italy, Greece and Africa and adorned with floors of black and white mosaics and murals portraying bath scenes. Roman public establishments offered two types of baths: therapeutic and hygienic. The baths at Cimiez were hygienic. They were accessed by a monumental gate opening into a colonnaded covered gallery which surrounded an outdoor pool. On arrival, a token gave admittance to the baths, and personal belongings were left in a cloakroom guarded by a slave. Clients were then free to practise differents sports, take a massage or proceed with a bath.

The West Baths within which a church-cathedral was built after the 5th century.

The Amphitheatre

The amphitheatre at Cimiez is one of the most significant relics of the ancient city of *Cemenelum*. Part of it has been well preserved. Standing seven meters high and oval in shape, it is comparatively small in size (69 meters long by 57 meters wide). Up to 4,000 spectators could be accommodated on several tiers of seating. Two monumental gateways situated to the North and to the South, gave access to the arena. Recent excavations (2010) have enabled the period of construction to be dated at the end of the 1st century A.D.

Earring with pearls, garnets and *lapis lazuli*, found at Cemenelum, on view at the Museum Nice-*Cemenelum*
(photo by D. Taland - Museum Nice-*Cemenelum*)

The Archaeological Museum

Exhibits illustrating life in the Roman city of *Cemenelum* can be viewed at the archaeological site museum of Nice-Cimiez, such as the wild boar in bronze plate from Ilonse retrieved during excavations, or objects of worship from the Temple of Mithras at Mandelieu and collections rescued during maritime archaeological explorations. The lower level of the museum displays funerary artefacts from the necropoli of *Cemenelum* and Nice and 5,000 documents are available for consultation by the public in the new library.

HOW TO GET THERE

The Museum and archaeological site
Address:.160, avenue des Arènes de Cimiez. Open from 10 a.m. to 6 p.m. Closed on Tuesday. Entrance free.
Tel : 04 93 81 59 57

Bus: N°. 15, 20, 22, 24 - Bus stop : Arènes
Bus: N°. 17, 25 - Bus stop : Monastère

The amphithéâtre
Located next to the entrance to the museum.

NICE, THE MEDIEVAL CITY

VILLE HAUTE & VILLE BASSE

At the end of the Roman Empire, the population migrated from *Cemenelum* to Nice which afforded better defences against attacks. In the 10th century Nice passed under the control of the Counts of Provence who had liberated the region from Saracen invaders. In 1388, conflict for the succession of Provence resulted in Nice placing itself under the protection of the House of Savoy while maintaining its autonomy and privileges. The town continued to grow and by the end of the Middle Ages had become an important point of passage for all of the hinterland.

WHAT TO SEE

The archaeological crypt, Old-Nice, the ruins of the castle

DATES

From the 6th century to the 15th century

The City on the Hill (*Ville Haute*) and the Town Below (*Ville Basse*)

The town of Nice perched on its hilltop (*Colline du Château*) continued to develop throughout the Middle Ages. From the 12th century, it spread north and west over the primitive defences and across the hillside. However, it was during the 13th century that its expansion was the most important engulfing land to the west belonging to the Abbey of Saint-Pons. In 1388, when Nice joined the House of Savoy, the population of the town stood at 5,000 inhabitants occupying both the upper and lower districts of the town. The members of the city's oligarchy (the nobility, lawyers and merchants), the *majores* who controlled government occupied the *Ville Haute*; the ordinary people, the *minores*, lived in the *Ville Basse*. When the hill was fortified several centuries later, the cathedral was moved down to Sainte-Réparate, completing the displacement of the civil population from the *Ville Haute* to the *Ville Basse*.

View of the the medieval Old Town from the *Colline du Château*

A WALK INTO THE MIDDLE AGES

Here is a short walk from Place Garibaldi via the maze of narrow medieval streets of Old Nice to the park on the hill (*Colline du Château*). Before leaving Place Garibaldi, it is worth visiting the archaeological crypt (see page 45 for information on reserving a guided tour) to get a glimpse of medieval Nice hidden beneath the tram line. On leaving the crypt, turn right in front of the Café de Turin and second left into Rue Pairolière (which used to lead to one of the town's main gateways, the Porte Pairolière). The facades of the houses have changed very little since medieval times. Continue straight on into rue Saint-François and left into Rue Droite, then right into Place Rossetti where the Cathedral of Sainte-Réparate stands. The cathedral was rebuilt in the 17th century on the site of a former 13th century chapel (see page 102). Turn left in front of the cathedral, then right and left into Rue Saint-Gaëtan. Cross the Cours Saleya which you exit via the last gate on the left. Turn left and go the end of the Rue des Ponchettes where there are lifts and steps up to the Park. The keep of the old castle was at the summit of the hill (where the souvenir shops are), from where the Governor of Nice could survey the town beneath, the bay and the hills beyond. Don't miss the archaeological excavations including Nice's first cathedral (see page 31).

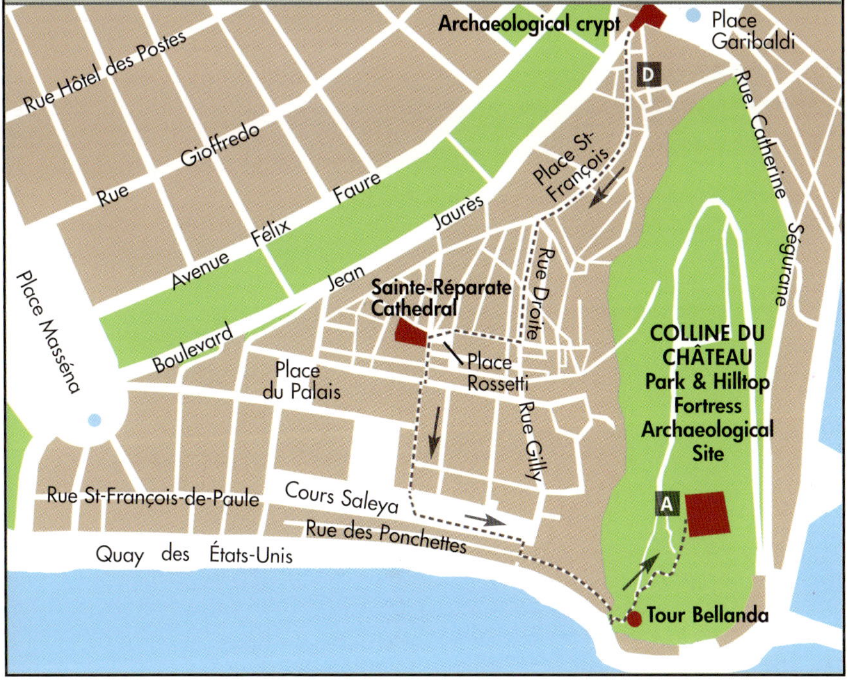

View of Nice by Balduino in 1610 - Archives départementales des Alpes-Maritimes

Nice and Early Christianity

During the Middle Ages, the presence of the Christian religion was perceivable throughout Nice where the Bishop was one of the most important public figures. The cathedral was located opposite the castle in the *Ville Haute*. Convents were either built outside the city walls (Augustins, Carmes) or within the town (Franciscans, Dominicans) and the *Ville Basse* was divided into parishes. The influence of religion on Nicois society is clearly seen in the wills that were made. It was common for large sums of money to be bequeathed to a convent, which sometimes inherited properties giving them a substantial income. The building of vast churches by the religous orders is also evidence of the importance of religion to the population. In 1404, Nice played an international role during the Great Schism between the Roman Catholic churches of Avignon and Rome when the Count of Savoy left the castle and the town of Nice to the French/Provencal antipope Benedict III.

The Castle (*Château de Nice*)

The castle which dominated the town dated back to the year 1,000 or earlier. It was destroyed in 1215 when Nice surrendered to Genova, and then rebuilt in 1229 to serve as a residence to the Count of Provence. By 1388 when Nice joined the House of Savoy, the castle had fallen into disrepair. It was rebuilt over the next few hundred years by the Dukes of Savoy and a citadel was built on the northern slopes. Important works were undertaken by the Governor Nicod de Menthon beginning in 1436 to reinforce the ancient city defences and protect the town against artillery attacks. As well as the renovation of the castle, a courtine was built to protect the northern side of the Ville Haute. Three towers punctuate the 2.5 meter thick wall. One, the central tower, gave access to the northern districts of the *Ville Haute*, while another provided access from the *Ville Basse*. As Tobias Smollett put it so succinctly only half a century after the demolition of the castle in 1706 by Louis XIV, "before the invention of artillery, (it) was counted impregnable".

Detail of an altarpiece by Louis Bréa apparently depicting the *Porte Pairolière*. The painting is held by the Dominican church at Taggia, Italy.

The Old-Bridge (*Pont-Vieux*)

The River Paillon to the west of the Old Town has always been subject to sudden devastating floods. In 2006, the archaeological dig uncovered remains of the bridge that was built during the 13th century to enable, for the first time, unhindered movement of people and goods over the river. The river played an important role in the town's economy, supplying water to the town's industries; milling, tanning and the manufacture of linen and hemp. As soon as the bridge was opened, a new district grew up on the right bank around the hospital dedicated to Saint-Antoine. During the 1543 siege of Nice by the Franco-Turkish alliance, the town made the decision to deliberately destroy the bridge believed to be vulnerable. It was rebuilt for the last time in 1565 and finally demolished in 1921.

THE TRAMWAY EXCAVATIONS

Excavations between 2004 - 2007 during the construction of the tramway uncovered medieval remains of the old bridge (Pont-Vieux) and the main town gateway (*Porte de la Pairolière*). This remarkable historic site is preserved in an archaeological crypt, unique in France, located below the Place Garibaldi (see page 43).

The Town Gateway (*Porte Pairolière*)

Archaeological excavations carried out over an area of 2,000 square meters under the Place Garibaldi and the Boulevard Jean-Jaurès uncovered the remains of the medieval gateway, the *Porte Pairolière*, and its entire defence system. The earliest occupation of the site dates back to the Roman period around 5th century A.D. During the Middle Ages, the gateway was protected by a wide circular tower surrounded by a moat. Masonry remains of a draw-bridge structure which spanned the moat have been preserved. Once over the bridge, a narrow road led to the districts on the town's outskirts (Saint-Augustin), Lympia (now the Port of Nice) and Villefranche (which served as port to Nice during the Middle Ages), or into the back country. It was around this time that the gate took the name of the street that led to it, la *carriera Pairolière* (*rue Pairolière*). It was one of the three gateways, together with the *Porte Saint-Eloi* and the *Porte du Pont*, in the city's medieval city walls. The gate's fortifications quickly became insufficient to keep out assaillants and, in the first half of the 16th century, a club-shaped bastion was built enclosing the gate (see page 43 for more details on the *Porte Pairolière*).

NICE AND THE BAROQUE AGE

NICE: A FRENCH EXCEPTION

Nice boasts a rich baroque heritage. Whilst 17th century France under Louis XIV preferred the classical arts, Nice and the Kingdom of Piedmont-Sardinia were caught up in the effervescence of a new artistic and architectural style. Like its capital, Turin, Nice was expanding rapidly and called on the great baroque architects of the Piedmont to renovate its medieval city on a massive scale. Nice's Old Town is home to a wealth of treasures from the Baroque Age which continued to shine throughout the Comté de Nice into the 19th century.

WHAT TO SEE
The chapels and churches of the Old Town

DATES
17th and 18th centuries

The Age of Baroque: the Historical Context

Baroque art originated in Rome towards the end of the 16th century. The baroque style spread through Europe and Latin America over the next two centuries and influenced all art forms. Described as the "visual rhetoric" of the Catholic Counter-Reform, it revolutionized the concepts of church liturgy and religious buildings. Space suddenly became a theatre stage for the baroque architect who introduced bold new volumes and geometric forms with flourish. The new approach to church interior decoration, designed to dazzle and impress, was quickly adopted by the wealthy for their private palaces: liberal use was made of gilt, marble, stucco, bronze, decoratively carved wood and trompe l'oeil frescoes. The purpose was to persuade visitors of the power and glory of the master of the

The Chapel of Our Lady of Mercy (*Chapelle de la Miséricorde*) on the Cours Saleya

— A WALK INTO THE AGE OF BAROQUE —

Nice's Old Town boasts an exceptional number of baroque masterpieces, several of which are open to the public. This short walk will enable you to see several of them whilst enjoying the special atmosphere of the old city. The walk starts at the Place Garibaldi (tram stop Garibaldi), cross the square (Chapel of Saint-Sépulcre – see page 78), turn right past the *Café de Turin* and second left into Rue Pairolière. Cross the Place Saint-François where the Old Town Hall stands into rue Saint-François, left into Rue Sainte-Claire and right into Rue de la Croix. The Chapel of the Holy Cross (see page 78) is on the left hand corner (1 Rue Saint Joseph). Turn right into Rue de la Loge and left into Rue Droite to visit the Palais Lascaris (see page 76). Continue along Rue Droite, then turn right into Rue Rossetti to visit the Cathedral Sainte-Réparate (opposite on the Place Rossetti) (see page 100). As you leave the cathedral, turn right into Rue Sainte-Réparate and left into Rue du Gesù to visit the Church of Jesus (see page 77) at the end of the street. Turn left out of the church, continue along Rue Droite, then Rue Gilly to visit the Chapel of the Holy Shroud (see page 79). Turn right across the Place Charles-Félix into the Cours Saleya to visit the Chapel of Our Lady of Mercy (see page 79). N.B. The chapels of the Penitents Confraternities are open for service and special occasions. Each chapel has specific days and times of visits. Please refer to WHAT TO SEE later in this chapter.

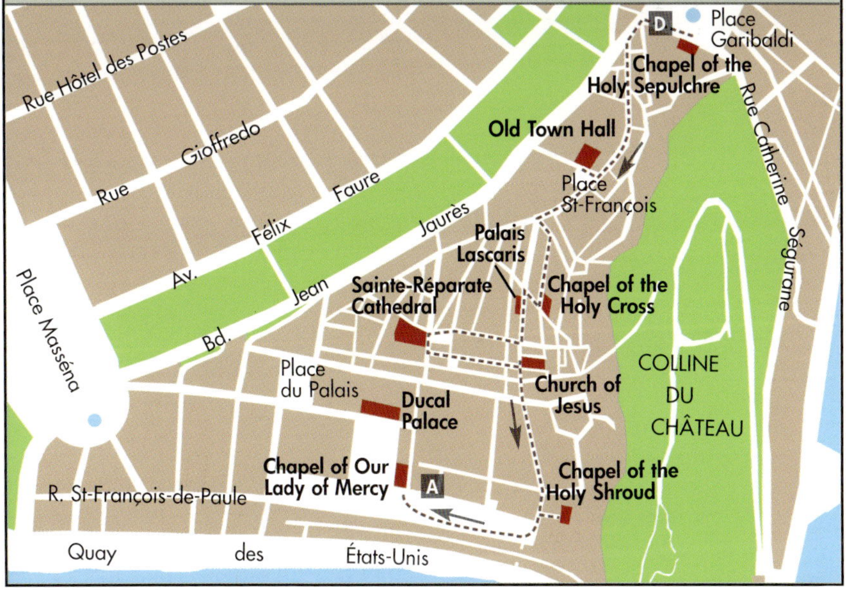

Monumental baroque staircases at the Palais Héraud (left) and the Palais Hongran (right)

house, be it God, the sovereign, the aristocrat or the wealthy merchant. Illusion, exuberance, movement, grandeur, intensity, exaltation, were the key words in baroque art.

The Baroque Palaces (*Palazzi*) of Old Nice and the Opera District

During the 16th century the hilltop town of Nice (*Ville Haute*) was transformed into a fortress. The civilian population was moved down into the town below (*Ville Basse*) where the Duke of Savoy also built a new residential palace in 1553 (*Palais de la Préfecture*), leaving the medieval castle its purely military function. During the 17th century, the aristocracy and the bourgeoisie built residences in the fashionable baroque style, such as the Palais Lascaris, or remodeled the interior of an old house behind its traditional facade. When the castle and the town defences were dismantled by Louis XIV in 1706, a new town (*Villanova*) was built to the west on reclaimed marshlands (today's Opera district). The plans were drawn up by the Royal Architect, Antonio Bertola, on the Turin model (a grid plan, with wide streets around a great square (*Place du Palais*). As space was not lacking in the new district, the great Nicois families invested in grand residences (*Palazzi*), reserving one or two upper floors for their private use and renting out the rest. Designed in the baroque style, they incorporated monumental staircases (*Palais Hongran and Palais Héraud*), palatial rooms, spacious interior courtyards and ornamental gardens.

The Palais Lascaris

The Palais Lascaris was built for the

Lascaris-Vintimille family in 1657. The facade of this *palazzo* is unique in Nice. Richly decorated in the baroque style fashionable in Luguria, it clearly announces the noble status of its occupants. By comparison, local *palazzi* owners limited any modernisation to the doorway and interior of their town house whilst retaining the more modest traditional Niçois facade. Visitors to the Palais Lascaris would pass through the imposing entrance door with its carved marble doorframe, and access the reception rooms on the second floor (the noble floor) via a formal staircase richly decorated with frescoes and statues. The Palais Lascaris was listed an historic monument in 1946.

The Chapel of the Holy Cross

The Old Town Hall (*Palais Communal*)

The construction of the town hall (*Palais Communal*) on the Place Saint-François was finished in 1581. The massive marble way door was added by Antoine Grigho a century later. Giovanni-Pietro de Tavigliano designed the ornate facade in 1758 in the style of Juvarra, the celebrated baroque architect from Turin. It would be in use as the town hall until 1868.

Baroque entrance door, Palais Lascaris

The Church of Jesus (*Église du Gesù*)

The first baroque church to have been built in Nice, the Church of Jesus was completed in 1656 for the Jesuit order. Its innovation lies in its layout which introduces new zones and redefines the place and role of each element. The sobriety of the rectangular great nave bordered by side chapels contrasts with the over-elaborate and rich decorations of the sacred space (high altar, choir and dome). The windows are cleverly set to induce surprising effects of natural lighting which draw the attention of the onlooker towards the heavens – and divinity – and onto the decorations (160 angels and cherubins). The Jesuits were extremely active in promoting baroque art as a way of broadcasting the Catholic faith. The church facade dates from 1825 and is inspired by the late baroque and neo-classical styles.

The Cathedral of Sainte-Réparate

For the history of the Cathedral of Sainte-Réparate please refer to the chapter on Nice and its churches on page 100.

WHAT TO SEE

The Palais Lascaris
Address: 15, rue Droite (Old Town). Tel : 04 93 81 08 08. Open from 10 a.m. to 6 p.m. Closed on Tuesday and certain public holidays. Entrance free. Guided tours on Fridays at 3 p.m. (5 €).

Chapel of the Holy Sepulchre
Address: 7 place Garibaldi. Mass on the first Sunday of the month. Open for visits on Tuesday afternoons from 4 to 5.30 p.m.

The Church of Jesus (*Église du Gesù*), Nice's first baroque church

Nice's Baroque Heritage and the Penitent Confraternities (*Confréries des Pénitents*)

Nice's baroque chapels have been owned for hundreds of years by Confraternities of Penitents (brotherhoods of lay Roman Catholics) whose members are dedicated to the public exercice of their faith and the tradition of charity (caring for orphans, the sick, the poor and the elderly, burying the dead, assisting prisoners and running a *mont-de-piété* or loan shop). Each brotherhood has its own coloured *cappa* (habit). Today, the Penitents of Nice continue to act as custodians of their priceless baroque heritage and participate in maintaining the city's traditional religious life.

The Chapel of Saint-Sépulcre (Blue Penitents)

The Chapel of the Holy Sepulchre was designed in 1784 by Antonio Spinelli as an integral part of the new Place Victor (Place Garibaldi). The interior of the chapel which is unusually located on the first floor, is a marvel of baroque architecture. Ingeniously contrived to give the illusion of height and space, the stage is brilliantly set to highlight the high altar and the sanctuary. The imposing chapel facade which catches the eye of the visitor arriving on the square, marries late baroque and neo-classical styles.

The Chapel of the Holy Cross (*Chapelle de la Sainte-Croix*) (White Penitents)

Attributed to the Nice-born architect, Jean-André Guibert, the Chapel of the Holy Cross (1765 – 1767) is a superb example of the baroque architect's genius. Skillfully placed windows induce a play of natural lighting effects which draw the spectator's attention upwards to the altar and to the heavens above. The pelican, the White Penitents' symbol of altruism, is ubiquitous. In this chapel the simple volumes emphasize the impression of soaring verticality; the faded greys and blues and the floral decorative motifs, rarely encountered in a religious building, convey an impression of harmony and light. The magnificent baroque facade and the decoration of the vault date from 1875.

A Red Penitent in front of the Chapel of the Holy Shroud (*Chapelle du Saint-Suaire*)

The Chapel of the Holy-Shroud (*Chapelle du Saint-Suaire*) (Red Penitents)

The Confraternity of the Holy Shroud (*Confrérie du Saint-Suaire*) has been present on this site since 1657. The original chapel, confiscated in 1792 by the occupying French Revolutionary Army, was returned in 1824 by Charles-Félix, King of Piedmont-Sardinia, to the brotherhood, now part of the newly formed Confraternity of the Most Holy Trinity. In ruins, it was rebuilt in the neo-classical style. The chapel is home to a remarkable baroque painting by the Niçois, Jean-Gaspard Balduino, rescued from the former chapel. Dated May 1660, it portrays Christ being wrapped in the famous shroud upon which the image of his crucified body would appear. Known as the Holy Shroud of Turin, it was in the possession of the royal house of Savoy from 1464 - 1983, which is why, in the 16th century, it was brought to Nice for safekeeping (1536 - 1543) by the exiled Duke of Savoy, Emmanuel-Philibert. Today, it is preserved in the Cathedral of Saint-John the Baptist at Turin.

WHAT TO SEE

Église du Gesù
Address: 12, rue Droite. Open from 9 a.m. to 7 p.m every day.

The chapelle Sainte-Croix
Address: 2 rue Saint-Joseph. Open on Tuesdays from 2.30 p.m. to 5 p.m.

The chapelle du Saint-Suaire
Address: rue Jules Gilly. Open on Tuesdays from 2.30 p.m. to 5 p.m. Entrance free (guided tour possible).

The chapelle de la Miséricorde
Address: 7 cours Saleya. Open on Tuesdays from 2.30 p.m. to 5.30 p.m.(Entrance 2 euros).

The Chapel of Our Lady of Mercy (*Chapelle de la Miséricorde*) (Black Penitents)

The Chapel of Our Lady of Mercy (*Chapelle de la Miséricorde*) on the Cours Saleya ranks amongst one of the world's five baroque masterpieces. The former Chapel of Saint-Gaëtan was designed for the Order of the Théatins in 1740 by Bernardo Vittone, the distinguished Piedmontais architect. It was acquired and restored by the Brotherhood of Black Penitents in 1829. Its interior decorations in the flamboyant baroque style were completed in 1876. The sacristy houses two chef-d'oeuvres, rare paintings of Our Lady of Mercy by Jean Miralhet (1429) and Louis Bréa (1515) of the Nice School of Primitives. The decoration of the choir and the sanctuary was carried out by the Nicois artist, Hercule Trachel in the 19th century.

NICE AND THE BELLE ÉPOQUE

SPLENDOUR AND EXTRAVAGANCE

The *Belle Époque* (1860 – 1914) was a legendary golden age in France. It was a time of peace, prosperity and creativity when important economic, scientific and technological advances were made. French fashion, cuisine and the fine arts flourished. During this period Nice also flourished thanks to a new industry: tourism. Its unique geographic setting and climate drew the aristocratic and artistic beau monde from all over Europe who stayed for the winter season, built grand houses and villas and contributed substantially to the affluence and modernization of the city.

DATES
From 1860 to 1914

Nice, Capital of Tourism

With an influx of tourists to house, Nice expanded rapidly with sumptuous villas, apartment buildings and hotels built in the fashionable *Belle Époque* style. Hitherto, Nice had been a Mediterranean-style city with its medieval Old Town and new districts set out in orderly fashion by the *Consiglio d'Ornato* (see page 22). Now, every kind of architectural extravaganza was permitted to please wealthy visitors such as Queen Victoria, the Czar of Russia and the Kings of Belgium and Sweden. Advances in civil engineering enhanced the city's appeal as modernizations such as the tramway, mains water supply, sewers and street lighting were introduced, while communications were facilitated with the construction of new roads and the arrival of the railway. The "Season" which lasted from October to April was one

The Palais Meyerbeer on the Boulevard Victor-Hugo

A WALK INTO THE BELLE ÉPOQUE

All over Nice are examples of buildings in the *Belle Époque* style. Here are three short walks to see some of the best :

Town Centre (1 h 30)
On the Avenue Jean Médecin you will see two banks : the Crédit Lyonnais (N° 35) designed by Sébastien-Marcel Biasini and the BNP (N° 35) by Charles Delmas. Close by on the Boulevard Dubouchage is the Théâtre de la Photographie et de l'Image (N° 27) (the villa's fine woodwork is worth seeing). The Musiciens district between the Station Nice-Ville and the Boulevard Victor Hugo abounds with apartment buildings and villas from that era. A short walk along the Boulevard Victor Hugo will take you past a number of examples. Turn right into the Rue Gounod to see the hotel of the same name (N° 3), then return to the Boulevard Victor Hugo where you will see the stunning Palais Meyerbeer (N° 45). Continue on towards the sea and the Promenade des Anglais.

Promenade des Anglais (45 minutes)
At the Promenade, turn right to visit the Villa Masséna (N° 35 – access via the gardens - see page 99) and the Negresco (N° 37). Walk back towards the city centre pas the West End, the former Hôtel Victoria, (N° 31), the first hotel built on the Promenade in 1858, and the Royal Hôtel (N° 23). Continue to the Opera House (Quai des États-Unis see page 85).

Cimiez (1 h 30)
Walk down the Boulevard de Cimiez from the Régina (N° 71 – see page 52) to admire the Winter Palace (N° 82), l'Alhambra (N° 46), Villa Surany (N° 35), and Villa Paradiso (N° 24), making a short detour on the way into Boulevard Édouard VII – the entire street is *Belle Époque* (see the extravagant Manoir Belgrano at N° 5).

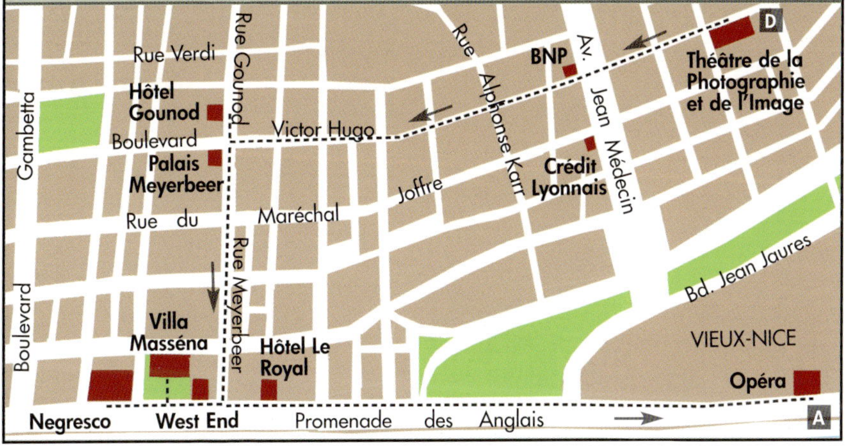

Villa Paradiso on the Boulevard de Cimiez

round of festivities with the Carnival as the high point. Between 1860 and 1914, Nice's population increased from 48,000 to 150,000 and the number of hotels from 35 to 200.

The Arrival of the Railway at Nice (1864)

Nice's central railway station *Nice-Ville*, (Avenue Thiers) was built in 1864. At the time, it was located outside the town in the rural Saint-Etienne district, amongst orchards and wild watercress streams. Designed by Louis Bouchot, for the PLM (Paris-Lyon-Marseille Railway) in the "Louis XIII" style favoured for many French public buildings; the station's slate roofs, bricks and stone made an eye-catching change of style in this city of the South. On her first visit to Nice in 1895, Queen Victoria drew into Nice-Ville on the Royal Train to be greeted by the Governor of Nice, a fanfare, enthusiastic crowds and one hundred and fifty journalists. The *Gare du Sud* (Boulevard Malausséna), designed by Prosper Bobin (1892), was the terminus of the narrow gauge railway to Digne which was built for strategic reasons given the vulnerability in wartime of the main PLM track that runs along the coast. The Nice-Digne railway is a marvel of 19th century engineering prowess due to its route through one hundred and fifty kilometres of mountainous terrain requiring twenty-five tunnels, sixteen viaducts and fifteen bridges. The station's great iron and glass canopy that covered the platforms came from the 1889 Paris World Fair. It has been dismantled for renovation. The passenger hall, which has been meticulously restored to its original condition, including the two splendid station clocks, is now home to the Raoul Mille Multimedia Library.

Cosmopolitan Influences

Three communities shaped Nice's urban expansion : wealthy British, Russian and French families built grand houses in splendid parks in a showy display of wealth and social rank. The former settled close to the Old Town and around the *Croix-de-Marbre* (New Borough), where the Anglican church stands today. The Russians gathered in the Piol, Valrose and Baumettes districts, whereas the French were dispersed throughout the town. The cosmopolitan mix was reflected in Nice's diversity of places of worship - Anglican, American Episcopal, Lutheran churches and a Russian Orthodox Cathedral (see page 95). The *Consiglio d'Ornato* plans prior to 1860 for an avenue which would link the new station to the Place Masséna (Avenue de la Gare), show a street with Italianate arcades in continuity with the Galéries Lafayette building (1859) and the Place Masséna. After Nice joined France, the town planners designed a "Parisian" avenue (now Jean Médecin) of plane trees and the *Belle Époque* architectural style was embraced unanimously.

An Architectural Extravaganza

The majority of the grandest houses were built prior to 1900. Some are accessible to the public today, such as the Villa Kotchoubey (the Fine Arts Museum – see page 99), the *Villa Masséna* (the Museum of Art and History – see page 99) and the *Palais de Marbre* (the Municipal Archives). Others, enrich the urban landscape with their majestic silhouettes : the Englishman's Castle or *La Folie-Smith* (see page 99), the *Villa Beau-Site* at the foot of Mont-Boron or the *Château des Baumettes* in the district of the same name, the *Villas Paradiso, Surany* and the *Manoir Belgrano* at Cimiez, the *Château Von Derwies* at Valrose (the Faculty of Science - see page 95). On the Promenade des Anglais, visitors can admire the *Villa Huovila* or the *Château Leliwa Rohozinsky* at Vallon Barla.

THÉÂTRE DE LA PHOTOGRAPHIE & DE L'IMAGE

L'Artistique (1895) was founded to promote Niçois artists and writers. Its success meant it had to move to larger premises several times (including one of the towers of the Casino Jetée-Promenade), arriving at its present address in 1910, a *Belle-Époque* villa on the Boulevard Dubouchage. A theatre was added and its programme widened to include talks, art exhibitions, concerts and gaming rooms, reaching a peak between the two World Wars with glittering receptions and well-attended conferences. It declined after the Second World War to be bought, in 1999, by the City of Nice to house an institution dedicated to the promotion and diffusion of the art of photography. Equipped with a library and research centre, it holds exhibitions and is responsible for creating a photographic inventory of the city : both new and old (its archives holds original prints (1863 - 1865) by Charles Nègre).

HOW TO GET THERE

Address : 27, Boulevard Dubouchage. Open from 10 a.m. to 6 p.m. Closed on Monday. Entrance free.
Bus: N°. 4, 17, 38 - Bus stop : Deloye-Dubouchage or Alberti-Hôtel des Postes or tram N°. 1 : tram stop : Jean Médecin.

The Casino Jetée-Promenade in its heyday towards 1925
Photo by Charles Nègre, Théâtre de la Photographie et de l'Image

The *Belle Époque* period saw the unprecedented development of grand hotels designed now for shorter stays and a new clientele of wealthy families E.g.: the Régina (built for Queen Victoria – see page 50), the Majestic (Cimiez), the Impérial (Russian district), now the *Lycée du Parc Impérial*, the Negresco (see page 14) (Promenade des Anglais).

The Casino Jetée-Promenade

The Casino Jetée-Promenade was the most singular construction to have ever been built on the Promenade des Anglais. In 1879, the Marquis d'Espouy de Saint-Paul obtained the concession on a plot extending out into the sea in front of the Albert Ier public gardens, upon which he planned to erect a floating palace dedicated to entertainment. Using the most modern materials and construction methods, he built a vast glass and metal domed structure to house a variety of attractions ranging from gaming rooms, a theatre, concert hall, bandstand, swimming and nautical clubs, restaurant and café. The Casino Jetée-Promenade was opened to the public on 1st April 1883, but three days later a mysterious fire completely destroyed the edifice. An eye-witness to the fire was the painter, Pierre-August Renoir, who was visiting an art collector nearby. He came across his older brother, Edmond, who was giving directions with "stupefying authority" from the roof of a car to a crowd of gawkers who were obstructing the fire brigade's access to the fire. Rebuilt in 1891 in a much criticised mix of modern and Moorish styles, the "Jetée" was nonetheless a tremendous success, only interrupted by the First World War. In the 1920's, Nice reached a new peak as a tourist destination with the introduction of the "summer season", which quickly became almost as popular as the winter season. Once again, the Casino Jetée-Promenade became a major attraction with galas, concerts, musical evenings and theatre. After the arrival of German troups in Nice, it was dismantled in 1944 for its copper (1,000 tons) and iron (4,000 tons) and its platform dynamited. Underwater archaeological searches of this important heritage site are currently under way.

Nice Opera House

The Opera House is one of Nice's legendary landmarks from the *Belle Époque* era. The site has been occupied by theatres since 1776. The construction of a royal opera by the city's architect, Benoît Brunati was launched in 1826 by King Charles-Félix. Brunati's design was inspired by the grand Italian opera houses which featured tiers of boxes around a horseshoe-shaped auditorium. The opera house was ravaged by fire during a performance in 1881. A monument to the memory of the sixty three victims who perished that evening can be seen at the cemetery on the *Colline du Château* (see page 104). A new theatre designed by François Aune who trained with Gustave Eiffel was inaugurated in 1885. He used traditional masonry with stone, brick and lime plaster/mortar, reinforced by an innovative steel frame. The ornate north façade with its pink Carrara marble colonnade, stained glass windows and statues of the Muses contrasts dramatically with the sobre white neo-classical facade at the rear.

Nice Opera House

The Craftsmen of the *Belle Époque*

The quality and diversity of *Belle Époque* architecture is impressive, as is the expertise of the craftsmen builders : masons, decorative iron-workers, marblers, potters, painters...Two architects, in particular, Charles Dalmas and Sébastien-Marcel Biasini, both Niçois-born, have left their city an immense *Belle-Époque* heritage of hotels, banks, apartment buildings, and villas.

HOW TO GET TO THE OPERA HOUSE

Address : 4 & 6 rue Saint-François-de-Paule
Tel. : 04 92 17 40 00
Tramway N°. 1 - tram stop : Opera-Vieille Ville
Bus: N°. 3,7,9,10,15,52 Bus stop : Jean Médecin
Bus: N°. 6,8,16,T26,38,62,88 Bus stop : J.C. Bermond

The programme of the Opéra de Nice offers a wide choice of concerts, ballets, contemporary and classical operas and performances for young audiences. The Opera House has its own ballet company, chorus and a philharmonic orchestra of 98 musicians which participates in national and international lyric festivals. Prestigious guest conductors are often invited. The Opera of Nice manufactures the costumes and scenery used in its productions in its own workshops.

NICE AND CONTEMPORY ART

AN ARTIST'S MUSE

Celebrated by the art historian, André Chastel, as a "huge art studio", the Côte d'Azur inspired the greatest artists of the first half of the twentieth century: Matisse, Bonnard, Léger, Picasso, Chagall, Cocteau and Dubuffet. In the late 1950's, Nice gave its name to the movement, "*L'École de Nice*" which continues today to generate its own dynamic across the world, contributing to Nice's international renown. It is fitting that Nice abounds with museums and exhibition spaces which pay tribute to these new talents in contemporary art.

WHAT TO SEE
The museums, galleries and numerous pieces of street art (see maps pages 6 & 8)

DATES
From 1960 to the present day

An Open Air Art Gallery

In 2007, the City of Nice inaugurated a series of artworks positioned along the new tram line. Fourteen internationally acclaimed artists, of whom four are Nicois, now have their work on show on the streets, radically changing the look of the city by day and by night. Three works were selected as *leitmotivs* over the length of the line: Ben's aphorisms in both Nicois and French on each tram shelter, Pierre di Sciullo's totems, and Michel Redolfi's highly original audio announcements in the tram. Visitors can also admire Jaume Plensa's (*Conversation à Nice*) on the Place Massena (seven statues representing the seven continents), as well as Michael Craig-Martin's frescoes "Cascades of Everyday Objects" (*Cascades d'objets du quotidien*) on the Boulevard Barel and Ange Leccia's "Solar Disk" at the Las Planas terminus which greets the approaching trams.

The "Square Head", Sacha Sosno

Sosno, Arman and Venet in the City

Works by these three major artists are dispersed through the city transforming it into an Modern Art Museum *al fresco*. Sacha Sosno designed the "The Square Head" next to the MAMAC, the first colossal "inhabited sculpture" in the world, which houses the administrative offices of the Louis Nucéra public library; the awe-inspiring "Venus" goddesses which adorn the facade of the Marriott Hotel (ex Elysée Palace) at 59, Promenade des Anglais and *Venus and Poseïdon* on the Avenue de la Californie. You can see Arman's Music Power at the entrance to the Acropolis Congress Centre (next to *La Tête Carrée* and the MAMAC). Don't miss Bernar Venet's uplifting sculptures which stand out in the urban landscape: "Indeterminate Line" on the Quai des États-Unis, "Nine Oblique Lines" which represent the nine valleys of the *Comté de Nice* next to the Opera House and "L'Arc 115°5 " in the Albert 1er public gardens.

The "Nine Oblique Lines", Bernar Venet

The Ferrero Gallery

In the 1950's, the photographer Jean Ferrero was close to some of the greatest artists of the 20th century: Cocteau, Picasso, Chagall, Miro, Calder, Man Ray... He supported the emerging movements of the School of Nice and New Realism, helping to promote these pioneer artists with films and photographs, buying their work and organising exhibitions and happenings on the 4th floor of his villa in the Mont Boron district. Their success led him to open the Ferrero Gallery, in the early early 1970's on the Rue de France, moving later to the present showroom on the Rue du Congrès. In 2003, Guillaume Aral took over the Gallery and continues to promote the artists of the School of Nice and New Realism, together with the new generation of local artists (Youn, Martinez, Bollié, Guerrieri, etc.).

Adresse : 2 & 6 rue du Congrès (next to the Palais de la Méditerranée). Open Monday to Saturday from 10 a.m. to 12.30 p.m. and 2.30 p.m. to 6.30 p.m. Bus N°. 8,11,60,62,52 – Bus stop: Massenet. Tel: 04 93 56 99 57.

Espace Soardi Studio

The Soardi Studio (*Espace Soardi*) was created in 1974 in the studio Rue Désiré Niel where Henri Matisse produced his first monumental work "The Dance" (*La Danse*) (1930 – 1933) commissioned by the Barnes Foundation in Philadelphia, U.S.A. Now established at a new address on rue Désambrois, the Soardi Studio continues to show the works of contemporary artists and photographers in an exhibition space of 200 square meters. In addition to promoting contemporary art and photography, The Soardi Studio also specialises in framing, preventive conservation and the renovation of period pieces according to museum specifications.

Adresse : Address: 9 rue Désambrois. Open Tuesday to Saturday from 10 a.m. to 12.30 p.m. And 2 p.m. to 6.30 p.m. Bus N°.15, 22, 30 – Bus stop: Désambrois. Tel: 04 93 62 32 03.

The MAMAC - See page 46.

Matisse Museum - See page 54.

Chagall Museum - See page 50.

The Villa Arson - See page 58.

LITERARY MEMORIES IN NICE

IN THE STEPS OF LITERARY TRAVELLERS

This chapter has been written by Ted Jones author of *The French Riviera: A Literary Guide for Travellers* and the *Foreword to Travels through France and Italy* (I. B. Tauris, London).

Since the arrival of the Florentine poet Dante in the fourteenth century, Nice has been a magnet for writers from abroad. Visitors don't have to look far to be reminded of them: from the rue Dante to the rue Smollett, city streets and squares announce their associations with pride. Nice is a treasure-house of literary memories. Generations of migrant authors, of many nationalities and genres, have found inspiration here: Tobias Smollett, Friedrich Nietzsche, Robert Louis Stevenson, Frank Harris, Anton Tchekhov, to mention a few...

WHAT TO SEE
The Old Town, the Musiciens and Buffa Districts

DATES
18th - 20th centuries

Tobias SMOLLETT (1721 - 1771) Nice's First Tourist

The Scottish novelist, translator and surgeon Tobias Smollett stayed in Nice from 1763 to 1765 when he rented a house at No. 3 rue de la Terrasse, (now rue Raoul Bosio). He wrote with enthusiasm "I am at last settled at Nice, and have leisure to give you some account of this very remarkable place" and "When I stand upon the rampart, and look round me, I can scarce help thinking myself inchanted". Asthmatic, consumptive and hypochondriac, he hoped that the Mediterranean climate would ease his respiratory problems. When his health improved, he used Nice as a base for his journeys into Provence, Tuscany and Rome. In 1766 he published his *Travels through France and Italy*, which became a best-seller of its day and

Tobias Smollett stayed at 3 Rue Paul Bosio. The house was transformed after his visit.

ITINERARY

Follow in the steps of our literary travellers through the Old Town of Nice, and along the Promenade des Anglais to the Buffa and Musiciens Districts.

Tobias SMOLLETT. This self-guided walk commences at the Palais Corvésy, 3 Rue Paul Bosio (formerly Rue de la Terrasse) - see maps pages 6-7 and 8. Smollett stayed in a house on this site from 1763 - 1765, "I have taken a ground floor... The apartments are large, lofty, and commodious enough, with two small gardens, in which there is plenty of sallad, and a great number of oranges and lemons." In 1768, it was transformed into a *palazzo* in the baroque style for the aristocratic Corvesi family by the Piedmontais architect, Filippo Juvarra. Its superb trompe-l'oeil facade has been recently restored. Continue towards the seafront and turn left to the Quai des Ponchettes.

Freidrich NIETZSCHE lived on the first floor of the house at 29 Rue des Ponchettes during the winter of 1887. Although the house is of little interest today, the Ponchettes and the view of the bay have not altered in essence since he wrote "The French part of Nice is insufferable, almost a blot in this meridional splendour, but there is also an Italian town – that is where I have rented, in the older districts, and when one needs to speak, it is in Italian; it is like being in a suburb of Genova." (*Letter to Peter Gast*, December 1883). Turn back until you reach the Hôtel Beau Rivage (1860) on Quay des États-Unis where Nietzche stayed in 1885.

Anton TCHEKHOV also stayed the Hôtel Beau Rivage, on his first visit to Nice in 1891 and again in 1894. Walk along the Promenade des Anglais. After the Palais de la Méditerranée turn right at Rue Meyerbeer, continue into Rue Gounod. Tchekhov spent the winters of 1897 and 1900 writing at the Pension Russe at 29 Rue Gounod. Now the Hotel Oasis, drinks are still served in the shady garden and visitors are welcome. Retrace your steps, turning left at Rue Rossini, right at Rue Alphonse Karr, left at Boulevard Victor Hugo, right at Rue Raynardi. Cross the Rue du Maréchal Joffre, turn into the Rue Longchamp (the Russian Orthodox church which Tchekhov knew well is on the corner), right at Rue de la Liberté, continue into Rue de la Buffa - **Frank HARRIS** lived for nearly ten years at N°. 9 Rue de la Buffa.

Tchekhov often stayed at the Pension Russe

Friedrich Nietzsche and Anton Tchekhov - the Hotel Beau Rivage

launched Nice as a tourist resort. An admirer of Smollett was Charles Dickens, who, as a boy, "read and reread" his novels, and praises them in David Copperfield. Two centuries later, in recognition of Smollett's contribution in placing Nice on the international tourist map, a grateful Nice put him on theirs, naming one of the streets near the port the Rue Smollett.

Friedrich Nietzsche (1844 - 1900) - Philosopher and Visionary

In the late nineteenth century, the streets around the port provided cheap accommodation for exiles arriving by sea and it was here, at N°. 38 rue Catherine Ségurane, that the German philosopher Friedrich Nietzsche rented a small unheated, uncarpeted room in December 1883. *The Will to Power*, *Beyond Good and Evil*, and much of his best-known work *Thus Spake Zarathustra* were written in Nice. His work has influenced generations of intellectuals. Nietzsche loved the Italianate splendour of the port and the old town - "The colours of Nice! I wish I could take them down and send them to you." He found the Riviera climate conducive to work "Like a plant, I grow in the sunshine", and he was to return, staying in a number of different residences, for the next five winters. In January 1888, he wrote home: "I should not fail to mention that this period has been rich in sweeping insights and inspirations for me, and that I have summoned up my courage to undertake the unimaginable and commit [it] to writing."

Robert Louis Stevenson (1850 - 94)

The Scottish novelist, essayist and travel writer Robert Louis Stevenson is best remembered for his novels *Treasure Island*, *Kidnapped* and travel publications such as Ordered South. He first visited Nice with his parents at the age of 12 in January 1863 when they stayed at the Hôtel Chauvain, beside the River Paillon. In the early 1880's, he returned to Nice with his Californian wife, Fanny. In October 1882, whilst searching for a home in Provence, the consumptive Stevenson rented a house, which turned out to be totally unsuitable. With his condition deteriorating daily, his wife sent him urgently to Nice, staying behind to pack. Because none of his letters or telegrams were delivered, she thought he had died on the way, and after four distraught days she went to Nice and tried every hotel until she found him... at the Grand Hôtel. After three weeks in Nice his health had improved sufficiently for him to renew the search for a permanent home, which he eventually found at Hyères. The following eighteen months were to be one of Stevenson's most productive periods.

Frank Harris (1856 - 1931) A Faithful Guest of the Côte d'Azur

The Irish-born American journalist and biographer emigrated to the United States at the age of 14. On his return to Europe he edited newspapers and magazines and wrote his four-volume autobiography, *My Life and Loves*, which was banned by censors in the USA and Britain because of its sexual frankness. As editor of the *Saturday Review* he was an early publisher of George Bernard Shaw and Oscar Wilde and wrote biographies of both. He moved to Nice in 1922. It was Harris who brought Oscar Wilde to the Côte d'Azur after his release from Reading Gaol, accommodating him at the Hôtel Terminus – "a tenth-rate hotel near the station". Harris remarried in 1927, aged 71, to his housekeeper, the former Nellie O'Hara, 31 years his junior, and died at his home: 9, rue de la Buffa, in 1931. Harris and Nellie are buried in a modest grave in the Caucade cemetery, just inland from the western end of the promenade. The memorial plaque in French outside Harris's apartment building reads, "Frank Harris, Irish journalist and writer and faithful guest of the Côte d'Azur, died in this house".

Anton Tchekhov (1860 - 1904) Patron of the Pension Russe

The Russian dramatist and short-story writer wrote hundreds of stories, but is best remembered for his plays. His most famous works include *Uncle Vanya*, *The Three Sisters* and *The Cherry Orchard*, which he wrote for the Moscow Art Theatre where he met the actress Olga Knipper, whom he would later marry. Tchekhov came to Nice, seeking a benign climate for his health, on four occasions, beginning in 1891, when he stayed at the Hôtel Beau Rivage. In leaner times Tchekhov and other impecunious Russians stayed at the Pension Russe, at 23 rue Gounod, now the Hôtel Oasis, in the Musiciens quarter of Nice. He finished Acts III and IV of *The Three Sisters* at the Pension Russe - while the actors in Moscow were already rehearsing Acts I and II. Tchekhov wrote at length to his brother Ivan about life in Nice. His letter written in December 1900 – "It is hot, the sun is shining, and the windows of my room are wide open – as are those of my soul" – was a cut above the average holiday postcard. His last visit to Nice was during the winter of 1900 - 1901.

NICE AND THE RUSSIANS

A LOVE MATCH

When one thinks of Nice at the *Belle Époque*, it is the English and the Promenade des Anglais that spring to mind, although the people of Nice cohabited with the Russian Imperial Family and the Russian community for just as long. The Russian legacy to Nice is remarkable: the Orthodox Church on the Rue Longchamp, the Saint Nicolas Orthodox Cathedral (one of the most visited monuments in Nice), and the Chapel dedicated to Crown Prince of Russia, as well as the Château de Valrose.

WHAT TO SEE

The Russian Church, Saint-Nicolas Cathedral, Chapel of the Crown Prince, Valrose Campus

DATES

From the 19th century to the present day

The Russian Community in Nice

All through the 19th century, Russian artists, writers and aristocrats, then several generations of Czars and their families were frequent winter visitors to Nice. Russia and Nice already enjoyed privileged diplomatic and commercial relations. Nice had a Russian consulate since 1783. A few months after the end of the Crimean war, in November 1856, Alexandra Feoderovna, widow of Czar Nicolas 1st, and her son, Grand Duke Konstantin, Supreme Commander of the Russian Fleet, arrived in Nice for the winter. Their mission was to promote friendship between Russia and the House of Savoy, and they were able successfully to negotiate the establishment, in 1858, of Russia's first naval base in the Mediterranean at Villefranche-sur-Mer. In 1859, the road linking Villefranche to Nice was improved and a telegraphic

The Château de Valrose, built between 1860 and 1870, is one of Nice's most impressive properties

THE RUSSIANS – THEMED WALK

For a short tour of the principal sites : Don't miss the opportunity to visit to the Saint-Nicolas Cathedral, which is an architectural treasure quite unique outside Russia, the commemorative chapel to the young Czarevich and take a look at the impressive Hôtel du Parc Impérial now a college. For a more leisurely tour of sites associated with the Russian community, do see Nice's first Orthodox church on the rue Longchamp and make the trip to the wonderful Valrose university campus – see page 95 (take the tramway to Valrose-Université, cross the square (Avenue Doyen Jean Lepine) and follow the Avenue Joseph Vallot to the gates of the Château). The fabulously wealthy Baron Von Derwies purchased a vast area of land to the north of Nice on which he built two mansions (one for his guests), a theatre-concert hall (he had a private orchestra) and planted a park in the Romantic style with grottos, fountains and hothouses. The Russian cemetery at Caucade where 3,000 Russians are buried (see page 107) is also worth a visit.

The Russian Church, Rue Longchamp

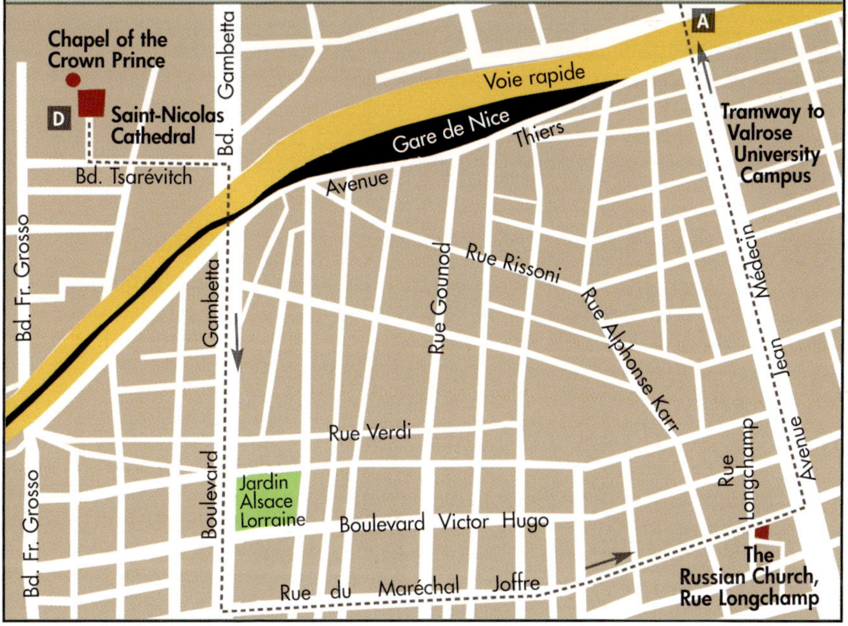

The Saint-Nicolas Cathedral built by Czar Nicolas II

"hotline" set up between the Russian Navy, the imperial family and the Navy's commanding officers in Nice.

The Czarina was immensely popular with the people of Nice. She donated large sums of money to hospitals and the poor of Nice and co-founded the first peoples savings bank (*Caisse d'Épargne*). During the Belle-Époque, the Russian community contributed significantly to the religious and cultural life and to the prosperity, of the region. The construction of the cathedral, luxurious villas and the Russians' opulent lifestyle generated wealth and employment for local businesses. The Hôtel du Parc Impérial was built in 1902 for the Russian clientele. Between 1904 and 1907, the *Nizza Express* train, operated on a regular basis during the winter season between Nice and Saint-Petersburg. After the Russian Revolution in 1917, Nice saw the arrival of the first Russian exiles, refugees from the political and arts worlds and ruined aristocrats, who formed a close community committed to actively maintaining and promoting Russian culture and the arts.

The Russian Church, Rue Longchamp

Whilst she was in Nice in 1856, the Czarina Alexandra Feodorovna, launched a project to build an orthodox church (rue Longchamp), deemed indispensable given the size of the Russian congregation. Commenced in 1858, the Church of Saint-Nicolas and Saint-Alexandra was dedicated to the Czarina and her late husband and consecrated in 1860. It rapidly became the centre of Russian religious and cultural life. The church contains a library which dates back to its foundation and holds many beautiful and historically important books.

The Saint-Nicolas Orthodox Cathedral

The Saint-Nicolas Orthodox Cathedral is the largest religious building to have been built outside Russia. Its architecture, unparalleled in Western Europe, merits its protection as an historic monument. The construction of the stately cathedral was begun in 1903 in the grounds of the Parc Bermond, the property where the Imperial Family stayed when in Nice, and which Czar Nicolas II had now donated for the project. It was inaugurated and consecrated in 1912. The cathedral with its reddish pink brick, pale grey marble and ornate cupolas covered with gold (the belfry) or decorative green, blue and gilded ceramic tiles, takes its inspiration from the highly unusual Church of Saint-Basil-the-Blessed in Moscow.

The Chapel of Crown Prince Nicolas Alexandrovitch

Close to the cathedral within the Parc Bermond, visitors can admire the chapel erected in 1867 to 1868 to the memory of Crown Prince Nicolas Alexandrovich who tragically died in his family's villa on this very site, aged only 21 years. He would not see the majestic cathedral, the construction of which commenced many years later.

The Valrose University Campus

Nice owes one of its loveliest, most gracious buildings of the Côte d'Azur to the Baron Von Derwies, owner of the Russian Railways, financier, engineer and patron of the arts. Château Valrose was built between 1860 and 1870. In 1957, after the Second World War, the City of Nice bought the property which was passed on to the State. Valrose is now a university campus which features amongst the best in France. It is the seat of the University of Nice-Sophia-Antipolis and the Faculty of Science.

The Chapel of the Crown Prince of Russia Nicolas Alexandrovitch

HOW TO GET THERE

The Russian Church
Address: 6, Rue Longchamp.
Bus: N°. 3,7,9,10,22 - Bus stop : Longchamp

Saint-Nicolas Cathedral
Address: Avenue Nicolas-II (Boulevard Tzarévitch). Open Tuesday to Sunday from 9 a.m. to 12 noon and from 2 p.m. to 6 p.m. (The times may be altered). The cathedral may not be visited during services. Entrance free. Tel : 04 93 96 88 02.
Bus: N°. 17,27,64,71,T75
Bus stop : Tzarévitch

The Chapel of the Crown Prince
Address: Avenue Nicolas-II (behind Saint-Nicolas Cathedral). Open Tuesday to Sunday from 9 a.m. to 12 noon and from 2 p.m. to 6 p.m.

The Valrose Campus
Address: Parc Valrose, Avenue Valrose. Tramway: N° 1 - Tram stop: Valrose Université. Bus: N°. 23 - Bus stop : Vallot

NICE AND ITS VILLAS

TREASURES FROM THE BELLE-ÉPOQUE

From the end of the 18th century a growing number of wealthy visitors from Britain, then from all over Europe, were attracted to Nice by its mild climate and dazzlingly beautiful natural surroundings and seascapes. They generally settled for several months over the winter, bringing with them their lavish lifestyle. From 1832, a new residential district of handsome villas and Mediterranean gardens emerged around the bay along the Route de France. It was dubbed "New Borough" or "Little London".

WHAT TO SEE
The Villa Masséna, the Fine Arts Museum, the Villa Furtado-Heine (facades)

DATES
From the end of the 18th century to the 1920's

The New Nice : 450 Architects and 20,000 Building Projects

After the Consiglio d'Ornato (see page 22) was set up in 1832 to plan and oversee the urban development of Nice, new districts began to appear amongst the farmlands to the west of the city. Thirty years later, the railway was extended from Marseille to Nice. Infinitely preferable to the long journey on poor roads, train travel was adopted from the outset by visiting foreign royalty and wealthy families, many of whom would, as a result, proceed to build luxurious villas in and around Nice. With the train came the beginnings of mass tourism. During the Belle-Époque (1860 – 1914) and Art Déco periods (1928 – 1939), Nice's population tripled and the construction industry boomed with 450 architects working on over 20,000 projects (hotels, apartments and villas). In the 1900's, the town spread

Villa Monhi at Cimiez (Boulevard Édouard VII)

THE VILLAS THEMED WALK

We recommend a visit to the Baumettes district, spending time at the Fine Arts Museum. Walk to the Villa Furtado-Heine (façades and garden only), both are splendid examples of "aristocratic" villas, and then visit the Villa Masséna (Art and History Museum) and gardens.

To access the Villa Kotchoubey (Museum of Fine Arts), take the stairs across the square from the bus stop Rosa Bonheur on the Rue de France. You will see the villa's magnificent façade ahead. After visiting the museum, cross the road to look at the Avenue Marie-Christine, then turn left down the Avenue des Baumettes. You will walk past several examples of *Belle Époque* villas set in their gardens with wondefully nostalgic names such as Fiorentina, Lézardière, Speranza (Nos 10 to 39). The Villa Furtado-Heine is on the corner of the Rue de France and the Rue Honoré Sauvan which will take you to the Promenade from where the garden and rear facade of the villa can be seen. Turn left along the Promenade past the Villa Guiglia (CUM - N° 65) to the Villa Masséna (N° 35).

Villa Surany (Boulevard de Cimiez)

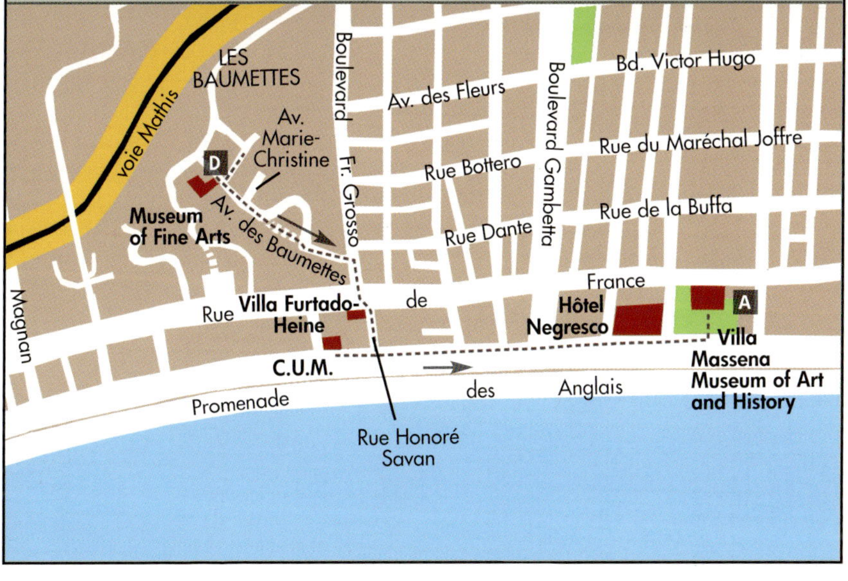

Villa Masséna (35, Promenade des Anglais)

into the surrounding hills, including clusters of artisans' houses with their gaily coloured façades and painted friezes (1920's). Amongst the few villas to have survived the post-war urbanisation of the Promenade des Anglais, the "aristocratic" *Villas Furtado-Heine* (1787) and *Masséna* (1901) illustrate the radical changes in architectural fashion and give a glimpse into the fabulous lifestyle of wealthy property owners in Nice during the late 18th to early 20th centuries. Other examples are: *Villa Kotchoubey* (Fine Arts Museum), *Villa Paradiso* (Conservatory of Music until 2006 - see page 82), *Le Palais de Marbre* (Municipal Archives), *Villa Guiglia* (CUM Conference Centre, 65 Promenade des Anglais), *Château Sainte-Hélène* (Museum of Primitive Art), *Villa Rambourg* (Romain Gary Library) and the *Château de Valrose* (Nice University – see page 95).

Villa Furtado-Heine

Lady Penelope Rivers, wife of an English Member of Parliament, had a grand neoclassical villa built on the Route de France in 1787. Its garden backed onto the seashore long before the Promenade des Anglais came into existence. Lady Rivers would abandon her villa shortly afterwards to the Revolutionary French army which occupied Nice from 1793 – 1814. Napoléon Bonaparte's sister, Pauline Borghese, would stay at the villa in 1807 and 1813. Changing hands several times, the villa's fate was fixed when it was bought in 1883 by Cécile Furtado-Heine, a German banker's widow and adoptive mother of the Princesse d'Essling (see Villa Masséna – page 99). A great benefactress, she donated it to the Ministry of War, in 1895, for convalescing officers. It is now a private hotel reserved for military officers.

Villa Masséna

This magnificent seafront villa (1901), built for the Prince d'Essling (grandson of Marshall André Masséna, ennobled by Napoléon Bonaparte for valour in battle), was donated by the family after the First World War to the City of Nice. The Villa Masséna houses the Art and History Museum (1792 – 1939) together with the Library of the Chevalier de Cessole (dedicated to the history of Nice, Savoy, Provence and Northern Italy). The ornate sculpted wooden panels that decorate the magnificent reception rooms on the ground floor come from the Govone Castle near Turin. The villa is truly impressive, as is the museum's collection of paintings, engravings and numerous objects which provide a unique insight into Nice's rich and complex history. The gardens have been restored to their original design.

Villa Kotchoubey

The Fine Art Museum (*Musée Chéret*)

The villa, which today houses the Jules Chéret Fine Arts Museum, was built in 1878 for the Ukrainian Princess Kotchoubey. Sold, unfinished, in 1883 to the American industrialist, James Thomson, it was completed by the Niçois architect, Constantin Scala, who added its handsome Genoese Renaissance façade. For over a decade it was the venue for glamourous soirees and concerts. The museum, opened in 1927, holds a large collection varying from 13th century regional primitives to 16th century religious masterpieces, to paintings by the Impressionists, designs of Carnival floats by Dufy and a unique collection of Chéret pastels and lithographs.

Le Château de l'Anglais (Smith's Folly)

The eccentric architecture of Smith's Folly (1858) was inspired by the mughal architecture of India where Colonel Smith had served in the British Army. Stephen Liégard, author of the travel guide *La Côte d'Azur* (1888) wrote that it could not be described as a castle, palace, tower, ... "or a wedding cake, or a Victoria sponge, or anything that has a name in any language." Converted into private apartments after 1945, it was listed in 2000.

HOW TO GET THERE

The Museum of Fine Art
Address : 33, avenue des Baumettes. Open from 10 a.m. to 6 p.m. Closed on Tuesday. Entrance free. Tel. : 04 92 15 28 25
Bus: N°. 38 Bus stop : Musée Chéret
Bus: N°. 3,9,10,12,22,23 Bus stop : Rosa Bonheur (access from the Rue de France a 5mn walk via the steps and through the gardens of the Museum).

La Villa Masséna
Address : 65, rue de France/35, Promenade des Anglais. Open from 10 a.m. to 6 p.m. Closed on Tuesday. Entrance free. Tel. : 04 92 15 28 25.
Bus: N°. 8,11,52,59,60,70 Bus stop : Gambetta Promenade

La villa Furtado-Heine
Address : 121, rue de France / 61, Promenade des Anglais. Now a private hotel. The facades can be viewed from the street and the gardens from the Promenade des Anglais.
Bus: N°. 8,11,52,59,60,70 Bus stop : Grosso CUM Promenade

NICE AND ITS CHURCHES

A DIVERSITY OF PLACES OF WORSHIP

Since the beginnings of Christianity, Nice has upheld a strong tradition of religious devotion and boasts a diversity of places of worship, many of which are architectural masterpieces, such as the spectacular baroque chapel (*de la Miséricorde*) of the Black Penitents at the heart of the Old Town and the exuberant Russian Orthodox cathedral built by Czar Nicolas II. The following selection (not exhaustive) of religious edifices is also of significant historic and artistic interest and well worth seeing.

WHAT TO SEE

Cathédrale Sainte-Réparate, Basilique Notre-Dame, Église Notre-Dame at Cimiez, Église Sainte-Jeanne d'Arc

DATES

From the 5th century to the present day

Church of Our Lady of Assumption (Sainte-Marie-des-Anges), Cimiez

In 1490, the Benedictine monks of the Abbey of Saint Pons built a chapel on the hill at Cimiez on the site of an ancient convent dating from the 9th century. It was sold to the Franciscan Order who founded a monastery in 1546. The church, dedicated to the Virgin Mary, our Lady of Assumption, became an important place of pilgrimage. The highly decorative"Troubadour-Gothic" facade by the painter and sculptor, Count Caïs de Pierlas, dates from the mid 19th century. During the same period the frescoes in the vault were painted by Hercule Trachel and those of the nave by Giacomelli. The church also houses three magnificent works by Louis Bréa of the Primitive School of Nice: Piéta (1475) representing the Virgin and Christ, surrounded by che-

The cathedral of Sainte-Réparate in the heart of the Old Town

A TOUR OF NICE'S CHURCHES

When you visit the Cathedral of Sainte-Réparate in the Old Town, we heartily recommend that you visit other churches of interest in close vicinity (referring to the map on page 8) : *Chapelle Sainte-Croix* (rue Saint-Joseph), *Église du Gesù* (Rue Droite), *Église Sainte-Rita* (Rue de la Poissonnerie), *Chapelle du Saint-Suaire* (Rue Jules Gilly), *Chapelle de la Miséricorde* (Cours Saleya) and *Église Saint-François-de-Paule* (opposite the Opera House).

For a tour (walking and tram) of: the Basilica of Our Lady (Notre-Dame), the Churches Sainte-Jeanne d'Arc and Our Lady, Cimiez (see WHAT TO SEE at the end of this chapter) : Depart by tram from Place Masséna (Direction Henri Sappia). Alight at Jean Médecin; the basilica is further up the avenue to the left. Then, continue on the same tram (Henri Sappia). Alight at Borriglione, walk up the Avenue Borriglione, take second right (Rue Charles Péguy). The Church Sainte-Jeanne d'Arc, is at the end of the street.

Cimiez : l'église Notre-Dame de l'Assomption

After the visit, return to the tram (Henri Sappia). Alight at Valrose Université, cross the square to take bus N°. 24 from the stop on Avenue Doyen Lépine (Direction Cimiez). Leave the bus at : Arènes – Musée Matisse. Cross the park to visit the Monastery, its church and gardens. While you are here, do visit the Matisse Museum and the Roman ruins in the park (see pages 54 and 69).

A haven of peace : the gardens of the Franciscan monastery at Cimiez

The Basilica of Our Lady

rubs, and two of his later works, the *Crucifixion* and the *Déposition* (Entombment). The magnificent gilded wood altarpiece of the high altar dates from 1664.

Cathédrale Sainte-Réparate

The patron saint of the city of Nice, Sainte-Réparate, was born in Palestine in 250 A.D. Put to death by the Romans, her body was set adrift in a boat and legends say that angels guided it across the ocean until it reached Nice. In the 11th century, a modest chapel was built in her memory which was enlarged during the 15th century. When the seat of the bishop of Nice was transferred from the Ville Haute in 1531, the chapel of Sainte-Réparate was elevated to the status of cathedral. This was demolished in 1650 to make room in the heart of the Old Town for a vast new cathedral designed, at the request of the Bishop Palletis, by the Nicois architect, Jean-André Guibert. Eight years later, building was brought to a halt by a tragic accident in which the bishop was killed by the collapsing dome of the nave. It was resumed between 1680 – 1685 under the direction of Marco-Antonio Grigho. The sober Genoese style of the nave contrasts with the elaborate decorations of the choir and the altar. The bell tower was built in the 18th century reusing stone removed from the site of the ancient cathedral on the hill (see page 70). The facade of the cathedral with the statues of saints and the medallion of Sainte-Réparate dates from 1825.

The Basilica of Our Lady

Nice's largest church, located on the Avenue Jean Médecin, between Place

Masséna and the railway station, is dedicated to Our Lady of the Assumption, as was Nice's first cathedral (see page 31). With the town's rapid expansion after 1860, the Bishop of Nice, Monseigneur Jean-Pierre Sola, felt that a church was required for the foreign communities and residents of the new town emerging in the districts between the Promenade des Anglais and the new railway station. Designed by the architect, Charles Lenormand, its resolutely French style inspired by the gothic abbey church at Angers, and its facade modelled on that of Notre-Dame de Paris, reflect the city's new political situation. Finished in 1888, the church was consecrated in 1925 and elevated to a basilica in 1978 by Pope Paul VI. In 2010, to commemorate the 150th anniversary of Nice's reunion with France, the basilica was restored to its original pristine splendour and a carillon of three bells custom-built for the Basilica by the specialist foundry, Paccard of Savoy. Two of the bells were brought from Savoy and the third bell was manufactured in Nice on the Place Massena during a spectacular three day ceremony.

The Church of Sainte-Jeanne d'Arc

Commenced in 1914, the construction of the Church of Sainte-Jeanne d'Arc was completed in 1933. It was the first church in France to be built in ferrocement (reinforced concrete), a technique which was perfectly adapted to its unusual design by the young architect, Jacques Droz, who used African domical huts as his model. The engineers Louis Pelnard-Considère and Albert Caquot, pioneers of ferrocement, supervised the construction of the massive oviform domes and the sixty-five meter high bell tower which is shaped like a twisted flame or Easter candle. The painter, Eugène Klementieff drew his inspiration from Cubism and Russian orthodox icons for his interior frescoes which represent the way of the cross.The church was consecrated in 1965 and listed in 1992. It was recently restored.

The Church of Ste-Jeanne d'Arc
Photo P. Behar

HOW TO GET THERE

The Cathedral of Sainte-Réparate
Address: 3, Place Rossetti
Open: Tuesday to Friday: 9 - 12 noon and 2 - 6 p.m. Saturday: 9 - 12 noon and 2 - 7.30 p.m. Sunday: 9 a.m. - 1 p.m. and 3 - 6 p.m.
Tramway - Stop: Cathédrale - Vieille Ville
Bus N°. 3,11,14,38,52,59,70 - Bus stop: Cathédrale - Vieille Ville

The Basilica Notre-Dame
Address: 37 bis, Avenue Jean Médecin
Guided tour possible: 9 - 11.30 a.m. and 3 - 6 p.m. (except Monday a.m. and weekends)
Tramway - Arrêt : Jean Médecin
Bus N°. 4,17,30 - Stop: Notre-Dame

Our Lady of the Assumption
Address : 86, Avenue Saint-Lambert
Open Tuesday to Friday: 9 - 11.30 a.m. and 3 - 6 p.m. (N.B. Friday morning: 9 - 10.30 a.m.). Tramway - Tram stop: Borriglione. Bus N°. 23 et T37 - Bus stop: Église J. d'Arc

The Church of Sainte-Jeanne d'Arc
Address: Avenue du Monastère
Open every day: 9 a.m. to 6 p.m. (except Wednesday, Sunday morning and during services).
Bus N°. 15, 17,20, 22, 24 - Bus stop: Arènes - Musée Matisse

NICE AND ITS CEMETERIES

PRESTIGIOUS RESTING PLACES FOR GREAT NAMES

Prior to the 17th century, the people of Nice buried their dead in the cemeteries of the Old Town (*Ville Basse*). The nobility and town dignitaries were buried inside the churches where they were believed to be closer to the presence of God. In 1783, King Victor-Amédée III signed an ordinance banning this practice which led to the creation of new cemeteries. These cities of the dead represent a precious record of the city's past and perpetuate the memory of the great names, such as Grimaldi, Matisse or Dufy, who changed its history.

WHAT TO SEE

The Cemeteries of the Château, Cimiez and Caucade

DATES

From the 18th century to the present day

The Cemetery of the Château

At the end of the 18th century, the site of the former hilltop fortress of Nice (*Colline du Château*) was derelict. The mighty fort and its defences had been dismantled in 1706 on the orders of Louis XIV after the war between France and the House of Savoy, and much of the stone reused for new buildings. It was the ideal spot to create new cemeteries as required by law for the Christian and Jewish faiths.

In the Christian cemetery, the majority of the tombs date from the 19th century when it became fashionable to commission an enduring memorial from a renowned sculptor. The most impressive of these masterpieces of art are to be found on the top terraces of the cemetery which covers the hillside. A microcosm of Nicois society, the Cemetery du Château is the last resting place of working-class families from the

A tomb at the Cemetery of Cimiez

ITINÉRAIRE PROPOSÉ

The three cemeteries of Nice are of great historic and artistic interest. The cemeteries of the Château and Cimiez can be readily visited in conjuction with other attractions as follows:

The cemetery of the Château is located close to the park on the hill (Colline du Château) overlooking the Old Town of Nice where archaeological excavations are in process of the former fortress of Nice and an early Christian Cathedral (see page 31). Exceptional panoramic views of the Port and the Bay of Nice can be enjoyed from both the cemetery and the park which also has a children's playground.

The cemetery at Cimiez is also on a hill with exceptional views of the coast. The district offers a wealth of attractions which can be visited on foot from the cemetery: the monastery and the church (see page 100), the Matisse Museum (see page 54), the Archaeological Museum of Nice-*Cemenelum* (see page 66), the Régina (facade only – see page 52), the Chagall Museum (see page 50) and the *Belle Époque* Palace-Hôtels (see page 80) on the boulevard.

Chapel of the Holy-Trinity, Cemetery of the Château, which houses the vault of the canons of the Cathedral. Mass is regularly celebrated here, together with the blessing of the tombs on the 1st November (All Saints Day).

The tomb at Cimiez of François Malausséna, 1st Mayor of French Nice (1860)

A Memorial at the Cemetery of the Château

Old Town, of Russian, English and American winter residents, as well of eminent political and social figures from the late 19th and early 20th centuries (their names are familiar from streets named in their honour – Benoît Bunico, Rossetti, Borriglione, François Grosso...). The style of tombs ranges from the Roman sarcophage, to elaborate architectural monuments with strikingly realistic sculptures in the Ligurian style and a magnificent memorial erected to memory of the Egyptian Ilhami Hussein Pacha. Opposite the entrance of the cemetery is the moving tribute to those who died in the great fire which destroyed the Opera House in 1881(see page 85). The Chapel of the Holy-Trinity (1935), to the right of the gate, was designed and decorated with frescoes by François Aragon, Architect of the City of Nice.

At the entrance to the Jewish cemetery is a cenotaph in memory of the Jewish victims of the Shoah who were arrested in Nice during the Second World War. In 2007, the road south of the Jewish cemetery was renamed the "*Allée des Justes*" (The Righteous among the Nations), and in 2014, a Wall of Honour was inaugurated in tribute to the men and women who rescued Jews fleeing from Nazi persecution. René Goscinny, the celebrated cartoonist and creator of *Lucky Luke*, *Astérix* and *Le Petit Nicolas* is buried here.

The Cemetery of Cimiez

Cimiez (*Cemenelum*), the capital of the Roman province of the *Alpes-Maritimae*, was founded on the route between the provinces of Liguria and Gallia Narbonensis, the Via Julia Augusta. During the 5th century, part of the ancient

Roman bath complex was transformed into an early Christian basilica, with a baptistry and a burial ground (see page 66). *Cemenelum* was abandoned in the 7th century. A chapel was built in the vicinity in 1490 by Benedictine monks that would later become part of the Franciscan monastery established in the mid-16th century. The Franciscan Order was granted the right to bury the dead: the nobility within the church and the people in a common grave. After these practices were banned by law in 1783, a cemetery was founded adjoining the monastery. Since the 19th century Cimiez has been considered the most elegant district of Nice and the tombs in this cemetery are those of the old aristocratic families of Nice and the foreign communities who had villas here. In contrast with the reputed affluence of many of the cemetery's occupants, many of the memorials are quite sober, often reduced to a simple tablet bearing their name within a family chapel: Caravadossy, Caïs de Pierlas, Orestis de Castelnuovo, Malaussena, Garin de Cocconato... The artists Henri Matisse (who lived nearby at the Regina – see page 52), Hercule Trachel and Raoul Dufy are buried here. The cemetery is well worth a visit, together with the monastery and its gardens – for their exceptional historic interest and an atmosphere of all-pervading serenity amidst the hubbub of the city.

The Cemetery of Caucade

Until the mid-20th century, the district of Caucade was still countryside covered with olive groves and the location of Nice's largest burial ground. The cemetery of Caucade is composed of three separate graveyards : the Catholic cemetery (1865), the English Protestant cemetery (1865) (now Sainte-Marguerite), and the Russian Orthodox cemetery (1867). The Russian cemetery, attached to Saint-Nicolas's Cathedral is privately owned, unlike the other two which are run by the City of Nice. The English and Russian cemeteries are of considerable historic interest for the famous artists, scientists, political leaders, ecclesiastics and princes who came to rest here. The very existence of these cemeteries is an indication of the size of the communities that once resided in Nice, particularly the Russian community which swelled markedly after the Revolution in 1917.

The English Cemetery at Caucade

HOW TO GET THERE

The cemetery of the Château
Address: Allée François Aragon (*Colline du Château*). Leaving from Place Rossetti (Sainte-Réparate Cathedral), go up Rue Rossetti to the steps (Escalier Eynaudi), then Montée Auguste Kerl (*Montée du Château*). At the top, turn left and enter the cemetery through the great gates across the road (see map page 8). Open every day from 8 a.m. From Nov. to Feb. closes at 4.45 p.m., from Mar. to Apr. and Sept. to Oct. closes at 5.45 p.m., from May. to Aug. closes at 6.45 p.m.

The cemetery at Cimiez
Address: Place du Monastère
Open every day from 8 a.m. From Nov. to Feb. closes at 4.45 p.m., from Mar. to Apr. and Sept. to Oct. closes at 5.45 p.m., from May. to Aug. closes at 6.45 p.m.

The cemetery at Caucade
Address: 7 Place Caucade (Nice Ouest)
Open every day from 8 a.m. From Oct. to Feb. closes at 4.45 p.m., from Mar. to May closes at 5.45 p.m., and from Jun. to Sept. closes at 6.45 p.m.

NICE CUISINE

A MATTER OF TASTE

Nice's cuisine is historically a poor peoples' cuisine in which tasty seasonal dishes are concocted with scant resources, dishes that are served as classic favourites or reinvented to surprise and delight. This is about knowing how to live well. Later, as trade exchanges between countries developed, Nice's culinary repertoire became more elaborate, cleverly assembling new commodities and spices... from the coastal trade between Nice and Genoa or exotic imports from across the ocean. Although similar cuisine can be found in Italy or Provence, there is at least one speciality from Nice (*Salade Niçoise*) that is known the world over!

Colours and Flavours at the

The market square in the Old Town is full of jovial banter, smattered with Niçois dialect, of vendors selling their produce. The laden stalls display a vivid array of colours : from yellow courgette flowers to deep violet eggplants and artichokes. Here, reigning supreme are fennel, garlic, rosemary, wild thyme, mint, and Swiss chard (used in the picturesquely named gnocchi *merda di can*), and *ballico*, basil for *pistou* sauce (brought to Europe from China by Marco Polo).

Delicious, Unassuming, Healthy Cooking

Nice's cuisine finds its ingredients in the market garden, with olives, especially olive oil, featuring in prominent position. The most popular traditional recipes are flavoured with its fragrant aroma. The classic favourites of Niçois cooking are : *salade niçoise*,

The market, Cours Saleya

ratatouille (summer vegetable casserole), courgette flower fritters, *farcis* (baked stuffed vegetables), *bagna cauda* (anchovy, garlic and olive oil dip which is served warm), *tourta dé bléa* (sweet chard pie), and the famous *pan-bagnat* (a round bread sandwich, "bathed" in olive oil and salade niçoise filling). Niçois cooks have always known how to garnish a bread base to make it simply delicious : *pis-saladière* (onion, anchovy and olive tart), bread slices spread with *pissalat* (*Peis salat* or "salt fish"), and sweet or savoury *fougasse*. Even the humble chickpea is transformed into the succulent *socca*, a sort of pancake cooked in a huge, shallow copper tray on a wood fire, finger food that is eaten hot with lots of pepper, or *panisses* (fried chickpea chips).

Food from the Sea

Nice has always had a strong fishing tradition and fish has a place of honour on its menus. Squid hotpot; fresh baked fish on a bed of tomatoes or fennel, and ravioli stuffed with red mullet. Stockfish, which northern sailors used for bartar when they called into the port of Nice, is used in the now typical Niçois dish, *estocaficada*. It was the sea that brought the *pomodoro* (tomato) to Nice via Naples where it arrived in the 1560's from South America. Believed be a poisonous plant with satanic properties, it was initially used to keep evil spirits away. Eventually, an intrepid cook came up with tomato sauce. It became popular when the Bolognese custom caught on of adding meat or when, simply spread on to bread dough and baked in the oven, the iconic *pizza* was invented. The tomato only reached the north of France after the French Revolution when a number of Provencal restaurants were opened in Paris.

Niçois Specialities

Mesclun (mixed salad) is made only in the Nice area. It is composed of dandelion, lambs lettuce, *riquéta* (arugula) watercress, chervil and purslane, and is said to have come from the monastery gardens at Cimiez

Socca

where monks gathered the green leaves and bitter shoots. The city of Nice also boasts a vineyard within its boundaries : the Bellet vineyard situated on the west-facing hillsides to the north of the town, where one of the oldest grape varieties in France is grown (probably dating back to *Nikaïa*, when Nice was a Greek trading post), wich was granted the AOC label in 1941 (Appellation of Controlled Origin). Nice's greatest culinary indulgence must be *li pasta* which in the Niçois dialect covers every kind of pastry, dough, batter and fresh pasta imaginable. Each village in the Region has its pasta recipe : *frigamoun* (pieces of raw pasta dough thrown into boiling broth), *lous andérouols* (pancake batter poured slowly into boiling water), *raiola* (ravioli) of every description... Visitors to Nice can enjoy local cuisine all year round. Restaurants serving authentic seasonal Niçois cooking display the Alpes-Maritimes Union of Tourist Offices Quality Seal: look out for the label "*Cuisine nissarde*" showing a woman in traditional costume carrying a basket of vegetables.

Where to eat

Many restaurants, bakers and grocers in the Old Town of Nice, as well as market stalls on the Cours Saleya (see page 26) offer typical Niçois dishes and delicacies.

WHAT THEY SAID ABOUT NICE

Nicolas POILEVILAIN, a visitor from France in 1405

"This place (Nice) is very pleasant and all set that we spend the winter here (...) The entire town is situated on sloping ground beneath a hill, on the top of which is a castle. From there, a beautiful, view sweeps across the sea and the countryside, unobstructed in almost every direction since with the gradient of the land, the houses drop away before you, laid out as regularly as organ pipes. All the houses, whether they are located on a hillside or in the plain, have a flat roof, which makes an excellent observation point. Commonly known as terrace, or what the Greeks called domata, they offer the advantage of being hidden from the sight of whoever is below. To the south of the town is the sea which, when the wind stirs it up, hits the ramparts, and to the north, at a distance of a little less than two miles, are the low-lying mountains of the pre-Alps. The plains that stretch between the town and the mountains are sometimes sown with crops, sometimes serve as pasture, and are sometimes planted with delightful gardens."

Letter to Jacques DE NOUVION, *Nice et son comté 1200 - 1580*, Éditions Mémoires Millénaires, 2010

Friedrich NIETZSCHE in 1909

"Many concealed spots and heights in the landscape around Nizza are hallowed for me by unforgettable moments."

***Philosophical Writings (Ecce Homo)*, The German Library, The Continuum Publishing Company, 1995**

Henri MATISSE in 1950

"When I realized that I would see that light every morning, I couldn't believe my happiness."

Quoted by Georges Salles in the Foreward to the Exhibition Catalogue *Henri Matisse, Nice*

QUEEN VICTORIA, May, 1st, 1899 (the last day of her last visit to Nice)

"Drove to Beaulieu. Had our tea at St. Jean... Alas! My last charming drive in this paradise of nature, which I grieve to leave, as I get more attached to it every year. I shall mind returning to the sunless north, but I am so grateful for all I have enjoyed here."

***Queen Victoria and the Discovery of the Riviera* by Michael NELSON, I. B. Tauris, London, 2007**

Tobias SMOLLETT, Nice, January 15, 1764

"When I stand upon the rampart, and look round me, I can scarce help thinking myself inchanted. The small extent of country which I see, is all cultivated like a garden. Indeed, the plain presents nothing but gardens, full of green trees, loaded with oranges, lemons, citrons and bergamots... green pease ready to gather; all sorts of sallading, and pot-herbs, in perfection; and plats of roses, carnations, ranunculas, anemonies, and daffodils, blowing in full glory, with such beauty, vigour, and perfume as no flower in England ever exhibited... Amidst the plantations in the neighbourhood of Nice, appear a vast number of white bastides, or country-houses, which make a dazzling show...The hills are shaded to the tops with olive-trees... and those hills are over-topped by more distant mountains, covered with snow. When I turn myself towards the sea, the view is bounded by the horizon; yet in a clear morning, once can perceive the high lands of Corsica."

Travels through France and Italy **by Tobias SMOLLETT, I. B. Tauris, London, 2010**

Ted JONES on SMOLLETT, Nice, January 15, 2014 (250 years later!)

"When Tobias Smollett arrived in Nice in 1763 aged 42, the Scottish surgeon-turned-author was already famed as a translator, historian and novelist. What is so interesting to contemporary readers is that until Nice was reunited with France in 1860, the border with what is now Italy was 10 kilometres west of Nice. In Smollett's time, Nice was Nizza, part of the Kingdom of Sardinia-Piedmont and the House of Savoy. Today, he is recognised as an intelligent and meticulous observer who left informed accounts of the region's cultural and archaeological heritage; its legal, judicial and administrative structure; its language, even its meteorology. Whilst Smollett was a self-confessed malcontent, whose criticisms of his host countries could be scathing, he could be equally complimentary. A thoroughly good read!"

Foreword to *Travels through France and Italy* by Tobias SMOLLETT

Ted JONES in 2014

"I was drawn the French Riviera by my earliest reading of adult fiction... It was these authors and their stories of azure skies and sun-drenched beaches that first aroused my ambition to visit this wonderful land where, it seemed, winter never ventures and the sun always shone. It was many years before I finally came to live in south-eastern France... I was fascinated to find that there were more reminders of its literary past than I had imagined and was surprised to find that no one – not even its resident writers – had attempted a literary history of the region. The prospect of travelling the length and depth of this most beautiful and fortunate corner of Europe recording its literary heritage suddenly seemed to me to be the most exciting adventure imaginable."

The French Riviera: A Literary Guide for Travellers, **I. B. Tauris, London, 2007**

ACKNOWLEDGMENTS

This guide would not have been possible without the help of the following:

Jeanne Augier	Owner and CEO of the Hôtel Negresco
Marc Bouiron	Director of the Archaeology Service of the City of Nice
Thierry Ciccione	StoA Architecture Associates, Marseille
Emmanuel Desclaux	Director of the Departmental Laboratory of Prehistory of the Lazare
Anne Devroye-Stilz	Curator of the Museum of Fine Art
Dominique Escribe	Former Attaché for Conservation, Masséna Museum
Jean-Marc Giaume	Councillor of the City of Nice for Historic Heritage, Archaeology and the Language and Culture of Nice
Monique Jannet-Vallat	Former Curator of the Archaeological Museum Nice-*Cemenelum*
Louis-Gilles Pairault	Former Director of the Municipal Archives of Nice
Gilbert Perlein	Curator of the Museum of Modern Art and Contemporary Art of Nic
Jean-Baptiste Pisano	Chair of Art History and Archaeology, University of Nice
Olivier-Henri Sambucchi	Deputy General Director in charge of Culture for the City of Nic
M. T. Pulvénis de Séligny	Curator of the Matisse Museum, Cimiez
Yves Robert	Former Director of the Villa Arson Visual Arts School
Bertrand Roussel	Deputy Director of the Archaeology Museums of Nice
Alain Ruggiero	Honorary Lecturer, Contemporary History, University of Nice

Françoise Gianelli, Dominique Counord (Théâtre de la Photographie et de l'Image Rebecca François (Attachée for Conservation, MAMAC), Bénédict Lacavalerie (Archaeolog Museums of Nice), Michel Maunier (Director of Communication, Villa Arson Visual Art School), Marie-Françoise Lauradoux (Personal Assistant to Madame Jeanne Augier Françoise Borello (Director of Communication and Development of Audiences, Musée Nationaux du XXe Siècle des Alpes-Maritimes), Gérald Griffon (Director, External Relation Hôtel le Royal), Nice Heritage Centre (Le Centre du Patrimoine, 75, quai des États-Uni Nice), Laurent Sigrist, Isabelle Vallauri, Morgane Boédec-Nesterov.

Special thanks to Ted Jones for his fascinating contribution, to Roger Berio (merci !), ISA, and across the Channel, to Linda Sakin and Robert Giles for their enthusiasm and good advice.

Translator and co-author of *Nice Le Guide*: Jane Bradshaw come from a family passionate about art, history, nature, wildlife and... everything abo France ! A great-great-great grandfather was a buyer for a London perfume hous and visited Grasse regularly in the 1850's. She enjoys hiking all over the Alpe Maritimes with her Niçois husband, Mémoires Millénaires' guide author, Roge Berio, as well as winter swims at Opéra Plage in the company of her editor!

Editorial Director: Frédéric Boyer - **Artistic Director:** Julie Michel (etag)

Printed by: Grafiche Diemme - **Published in (*Dépôt légal*):** (april) avril 2014

ISBN: 978-2-919056-33-0

 Photo Credits: Roger Bério, Mémoires Millénaires unless otherwise stated. Mapping: Mémoires Millénaires

www.memoiresmillenaires.com